Praise for Mimi
and *Activate Your*

'A powerful and special book that will move
you to create your finest life.'

**ROBIN SHARMA, #1 BEST-SELLING AUTHOR
OF *THE WEALTH MONEY CAN'T BUY***

'This book offers a practical application of mystical
wisdom. Activate Your Future Self is a must-read for
anyone ready to take their life to the next level.'

**GABBY BERNSTEIN, #1 *NEW YORK TIMES* BEST-SELLING
AUTHOR OF *THE UNIVERSE HAS YOUR BACK***

'I've been practicing "Future Self" work for over 20 years
now, and it's one of the most powerful methods for attracting
abundance in all areas of life. Activate Your Future Self contains
a step-by-step approach to use your mind, emotions and energy
to unlock and step into the life you've always dreamed of.'

**OLIVER NIÑO, #1 BEST-SELLING AUTHOR
OF *SPIRITUAL ACTIVATOR***

'Mimi simplifies what so many overcomplicate: how to become the
person you were always meant to be. This book is a game-changer
for anyone looking to create lasting success and happiness.'

JOHN ASSARAF, *NEW YORK TIMES* BEST-SELLING AUTHOR

'With Mimi's guidance, you'll not only imagine your
dream life but also take the actionable steps to achieve
it. This book is a game-changer for personal growth.'

WHITNEY PORT, CREATIVE DIRECTOR AND DESIGNER

'Mimi's approach to manifesting the life you want is a breath of fresh air. She tackles life's problems from the very core of the root issue instead of just making more noise in a saturated market. The Bounce Back Rate™ is going to help many people and is a concept I fully vouch for.'

NICOLE VIGNOLA, NEUROSCIENTIST AND AUTHOR OF *REWIRE*

'Mimi offers simple, actionable advice that helps readers bounce back after hardship and changes in their lives.'

ELIZABETH EARNSHAW, AUTHOR OF *I WANT THIS TO WORK*

ACTIVATE YOUR FUTURE SELF

ACTIVATE YOUR FUTURE SELF

The Secret to Effortlessly Becoming the
Happiest, Healthiest and Wealthiest You

MIMI BOUCHARD

HAY HOUSE

Carlsbad, California • New York City
London • Sydney • New Delhi

Published in the United States by: Hay House LLC, www.hayhouse.com® •
P.O. Box 5100, Carlsbad, CA, 92018-5100

A catalogue record for this book is available from the British Library.

Tradepaper ISBN: 978-1-4019-8025-2
E-book ISBN: 978-1-83782-323-9
Audiobook ISBN: 978-1-83782-322-2

10 9 8 7 6 5 4 3 2 1

Printed in the United States of America

This product uses responsibly sourced papers, including recycled materials
and materials from other controlled sources.

The authorized representative in the EU for product safety and compliance
is Penguin Random House Ireland, Morrison Chambers, 32 Nassau Street,
Dublin D02 YH68, Ireland. https://eu-contact.penguin.ie

To my younger self, who dreamed big
and believed in the magic of life.

This is all for you.

Contents

Introduction

Imagine this... you wake up one morning in your old age and are suddenly acutely aware that you don't have much time left on this Earth. In a moment of quiet introspection, you begin to look back on your life, pondering everything that's brought you to where you are today. You can't help but wonder how it would have turned out if you'd chosen a different path or made certain changes.

As you reflect, you realize that the person you are today is the product of the life you've lived. Has your journey been a fulfilling one? Have you reached your full potential? Or have you settled for mediocrity? As you look back, are you filled with pride and satisfaction or regret and shame?

A retrospective analysis of your life so far might show you the person you *could* have become. But what if you could meet a different version of yourself now: a fulfilled and motivated you who *did* decide to make changes, to do things differently, and to live out your potential? A version who chose to listen to that little voice deep inside whispering, 'There's more out there for you.'

If the prospect of not living up to your potential makes you feel unsettled, and if you're truly determined to transform your life and unlock the full extent of what you can achieve, then this book is for you. It doesn't matter *where* you're starting from. It doesn't matter *how* unattainable your ideal future *feels*. What *does* matter is making the decision to become your best self *now*, in this moment.

My Story

Right now, you already have everything it takes to make your dream life happen. You only get one life on Earth. Stop waiting for the perfect moment. Stop procrastinating. The time to act is now. Those exact words were flowing through my head on the cold winter's night nine years ago when I finally understood that my potential in life was limitless, and fully up to me.

What if we all have unlimited potential that we simply haven't learned how to tap into? What if our future holds a life greater than in our wildest dreams? What if we could earn millions of dollars every year, live wherever we want, enjoy a beautiful relationship with the love of our life, live effortlessly in the healthiest body imaginable, and help hundreds of thousands of souls with our life's work? What if...?

As I lay in bed in my 150-square-foot university dorm room, these 'what ifs' were keeping me awake. I thought about all the possibilities I could experience in my future, and I asked myself repeatedly: *If anything were possible, what would I want? What's the best outcome of my life? How can I achieve my dreams?* Somehow, I felt inspired by the fact that I was so far away from achieving these dreams. As a deep hunger grew within me, I realized that my perspective, the way I viewed myself and the world, would never be the same. An upgraded internal standard had shifted my mental gears. I now had a target, a goal: to fulfill my ultimate potential. Suddenly, nothing else seemed to matter.

This epiphany didn't occur in isolation. Growing up in Toronto, Canada, the child of struggling artists, I always had the sense that I existed on the fringes of a different, 'bigger' life. Although my family was surrounded by people with money and financial freedom, I never experienced this firsthand at home. We were always on the outside looking in. While our friends and acquaintances seemed to attract wealth and success, at times, we barely made ends meet.

There were polarities in my upbringing. My grandparents had some money, so they'd support my parents financially on occasion, for example, when they couldn't afford summer camp or extracurricular activities. This was done in a hush-hush way, though, and my parents felt ashamed about receiving help. I was aware of this because I'd eavesdrop on their conversations, hiding behind the second-floor banister in our small semi-detached house.

My grandparents' funds weren't limitless, however, and my parents were forced to remortgage the house several times. There was also a bankruptcy that created intense pressure for the family when I was young. Later, money and financial freedom became incredibly important to me, because I'd witnessed the stress and health problems that plagued my parents from a lack of it. In fact, money was the only thing my parents really fought about, and those disputes, often charged with desperation and other strong emotions, left a lasting impression on me. I was determined to earn enough money to never again experience financial stress and thus committed to creating a different life for myself and my parents.

Beyond the financial struggles of my childhood, when I was around eight years old, I became extremely self-conscious, constantly worrying about my body and how I looked. When

I was 12, in a restaurant bathroom as our moms sat at a table nearby, a friend taught me how to throw up the food I'd just eaten. I was very impressionable at that age, and this incident marked the beginning of an eating disorder that would resurface sporadically over the next eight years.

I faced many other challenges between the ages of 12 and 18, including a period of intense personal struggle that involved self-harm and depression. I had problems around self-love, confidence, and 'fitting in.' Yet these very challenges are what shaped my deep desire to become more and seek a healthier mindset; they fueled me to transcend my circumstances. I don't think back on that period of my life often, but when I do, I'm reminded that everything that happens to us serves a purpose. These difficult experiences during my formative years allowed me to grasp and appreciate a wide range of emotions in a way that I never would have done otherwise. I also embraced personal development with an intense passion, committing to a path of growth and self-improvement that's fundamentally defined the person I am today and has helped me to create a successful life before reaching the age of 30.

At 18, I began to see the light at the end of the tunnel. I left behind my old life in the home where I'd grown up, driven by an inner belief that there was more for me – more to become, to live, and to experience. Though I got a partial scholarship at a Canadian university, I dropped out after the first semester, moved to London in the UK, and began my entrepreneurial journey at the age of 19. By February 2016, there was just $9.63 remaining in my bank account, and as a result, I became a true hustler – working four jobs, trying to make ends meet while putting in late nights on my first entrepreneurial venture, an online magazine.

My Transformation Begins

This was around the time in my life when everything began to change. *The Success Principles* by Jack Canfield fell into my hands, and with it came the realization that I was capable of much more. Canfield's book (along with the many others I read subsequently) and a combination of life lessons from my mentors and my own experiences have guided me to my current success.

I've learned a set of principles through personal discovery, mentorship, and a relentless pursuit of growth, tapping into every resource possible, including books, courses, and podcasts. By living through these lessons, I've figured out what truly works.

Which brings us to now. At the age of 28, I can honestly say that my life is something formed from my wildest dreams. Although I've had numerous failures along the way, I've moved very fast over the past decade and have experienced many extremes:

- From having $9 in my bank account to being worth $40m today.

- From being single and lonely to finding and marrying my soulmate.

- From feeling deep insecurity to embodying pure confidence every single day.

- From being constantly confused to having crystal-clear clarity about my true purpose.

- From making zero impact in the world to changing hundreds of thousands of lives.

- From having a serious eating disorder to enjoying a healthy physique and body image.

Every area of my life has been radically transformed. I'm finally living my purpose. I feel more like the true essence of *me* than ever before, and finally, there's no confusion or resistance. How did I achieve all this? By aligning with the energy of the life I desired, changing my self-image, behaviors, and mindset, and activating and becoming my ultimate 'Future Self.'

I can tell you with absolute certainty that you have more potential within you than you ever thought possible. What you can accomplish over the next two, five, or 10 years has no ceiling. Your dreams and goals are limitless. This book, with its simple but powerful insights, tools, and strategies, will help you to identify what you really want, and then guide you through your transformation into *your* Future Self – the ultimate version of you who's living the life you've always longed for.

Every aspect of your life will start to shift – from your health and your relationships to your career and your finances – and it may happen faster than you're prepared for. But don't worry, I'm going to walk you through the entire process. It will be amazing. You're going to reconnect with your truest, most authentic self and step into who you were always meant to be; the person your soul was craving to become from the moment you were born.

Taking Ownership of Your Life

Before you dive any further into this book, it's essential to understand a principle that will be critical to your future success: *You are 100 percent responsible for your life*. This is a difficult idea to accept, and it can be triggering at first. But in time, it becomes an empowering core belief within you. Truly recognizing and embracing the truth of it will open your mind to a whole new world.

You are responsible for this beautiful life that you've been given the chance to live – for the thoughts you have, the beliefs you embody, the actions you take, the habits you commit to. It's essential to take ownership of your life and embrace this responsibility. When you do, you empower yourself to make the necessary changes and take intentional steps toward your goals.

When you shift to this new mindset, you'll no longer rely on external factors or blame others for your circumstances. Instead, you'll take control of your life and create the reality you desire. You are the captain of your ship, and the direction you take is entirely up to you. You can truly achieve anything and everything you've ever wanted. Remember that every monumental achievement starts with the decision to try.

Whatever's happened in the past doesn't matter. What does matter is how you decide to change things from this moment on. The narrative of your life is determined by the actions and choices you make today. I'll show you how to let go of the 'what ifs' from your past and focus on the potential of your Future Self.

You're Not a Victim

We're living in a time when it's all too easy to slip into the role of victim. Many of us succumb to narratives of self-limitation and blame that are tethered to restrictive beliefs such as 'The best opportunities always pass me by.' Or 'I come from the wrong kind of background, so I can't achieve much.' These beliefs are seductive because they absolve us of responsibility. But they're also chains that bind us to a stagnant life.

Yes, the playing field isn't level, and life is unfair. However, a less than favorable starting point doesn't make our goals and dreams impossible to achieve; it might just mean we'll have a longer journey to get there. There are countless people who started from a difficult place or faced tough challenges and yet still attained success and happiness. Let's move past these perceived obstacles and stop lying to ourselves; I'm here not to perpetuate these limiting narratives but to help you break them down. You deserve to know the truth. You deserve to see the real potential you hold.

Victims see limits. Creators see possibility. Decide to be a creator.

Every challenge provides us with two options: stay passive and complain or take charge and change. Choose to take charge and be proactive, because every challenge is an opportunity in disguise. I'll say it again: *You are 100 percent responsible for your life.* Allow this truth to empower you, because it means your future is fully in your hands.

Now *feel* the excitement that this new belief brings. It's a liberating thing, being 100 percent responsible for your life! When you believe that you're the *creator* of your life, you become deeply empowered to envision whatever it is your heart desires. No person, no thing, and no circumstances can prevent you from creating the future you desire. It's up to you. How beautiful is that?

How This Book Works

Activate Your Future Self is organized into three sections.

- Part I is all about gaining *Clarity* on what your ideal life looks like and what you really want. I'll show you how to craft a detailed vision of your Future Self – the person you aspire to become – and then draw on your unique Future Self frequency to fuel that vision. You'll also learn how to live as your Future Self now, in the present.

- Part II guides you into *Becoming* your Future Self. We'll review the neuroscience behind how your thoughts and beliefs shape your reality; explore why cultivating a powerful self-image is crucial to your transformation; and look at ways to hack your environment and your decision-making as you embody your Future Self.

- Part III provides support in *Maintaining* your Future Self transformation. We'll look at the optimal morning routine and I'll help you see that it's better to be adaptable than perfect. You'll also learn how to utilize the Bounce Back Rate™ – my tool for strengthening resilience and the ability to recover from failure and setbacks.

Authors writing on personal development will typically present a single explanation or concept in their work, whether it's based on psychology, science, spirituality, or quantum physics. But I'm taking a different approach in this book.

I'm intentionally sharing a diverse range of perspectives and thought, from the scientific to the spiritual, because I believe that the intersection of these disciplines offers a richer understanding of how our inner world shapes our reality and how we can change ourselves and our lives for the better.

My goal is to motivate and inspire you to action. So, are you ready to activate your Future Self and start living your dream life right now?

PART I

CLARITY

In this first part of the book, we'll explore the foundational step in your journey of transformation: achieving clarity about the person you truly want to become and the life you want to live. To transform, you first need a clear, detailed vision of your Future Self – an evolved version of you who embodies everything you desire, from success and good health to happiness. By taking the time to fully recognize who your ideal Future Self is, you open yourself to exponential growth and begin to experience the life you were meant to live.

This is where it all begins – getting clear on who you're meant to be and then setting yourself on the path to becoming that person.

CHAPTER 1

Meet Your Future Self

My personal development journey began almost a decade ago, but the most significant changes have occurred in the past five years, as I've finally figured out and focused on the principles, practices, and habits for success that really work. I've learned that as well as taking full responsibility for our life, we need to be adaptable, maintain an unwavering belief in our potential, and be willing to take bold steps, even when the path ahead isn't perfectly laid out. And most importantly, we must reflect deeply on what we truly want in life and who we want to be, and then embrace the truth that we have the power to create any reality we envision.

The high-level practice that ignited my transformation was envisioning my ideal life and the person I aspired to become – my 'Future Self' – and then acting and feeling like her, *being her*, in the *present moment*, as often as possible, especially while doing small, everyday activities.

And whenever I fell off track and reverted to being like my 'Old Self' – the one that's stuck in unhelpful or harmful habits, limiting beliefs, and routines that no longer serve me – I focused on quickly realigning with the qualities of my Future Self (I call this Bouncing Back and I'll show you how to do it in Part III). I also became uncompromising about surrounding myself with people, places, and things that matched the future I was creating.

Connecting with and then activating my Future Self in this way has reshaped every aspect of my life for the better and propelled me toward my dreams, and it can do the same for you. Let me explain how I discovered this dynamic and evolving practice.

A Life-Changing Discovery

When I first decided to act on my deep desire to transform my life, I discovered that I couldn't stick to the one thing that all the successful self-help experts told me to do: meditate. I tried. I really did. But I found traditional meditation boring and frustrating. Listening to a stranger's monotone voice through my headphones while I attempted to clear my mind felt disconnected from my goal-driven nature. Plus, finding 20 minutes or more every day to meditate was tough while juggling four jobs and striving to make my dreams a reality. Meditation didn't make me feel any different, and I craved listening to something that would invigorate me, immediately shift my state, and help me reach my goals.

So, inspired by my passion for audio and a strong interest in the power of visualization from the perspective of both neuroscience and spirituality, I decided to create something that *would* meet my needs. Using the voice memo app on my phone I recorded the first Activation - a vivid description of my ideal life and all that I'd achieved in it. I included affirmations and motivational words, and crucially, I spoke about this life and the version of me who was living it - my Future Self - as if they were *already* my reality. I described the qualities of the man I was married to;

how it felt to earn millions of dollars; the joy of loving my body and being healthy.

I then played this audio recording every day as I went about my life – while getting ready to go out, sitting on public transport, working out at the gym, cooking a meal, and so on – and as I listened, I visualized myself living as my Future Self *right there and then.*

After a few weeks, I grew bored of the original audio, so I recorded a new one. And then another. A long-time believer in the transformative power of music, eventually, I began using a professional microphone and the GarageBand app to layer in inspiring music from YouTube, which I discovered turbocharged the effects of my audios.

As the years passed, I created dozens of these voice and music memos. Some were general; others were more specific. It became my favorite personal development practice. The crazy part? I began to notice dramatic advancements in my life; I'm certain that before I started listening to these audios, the pace of my improvement was much slower.

Three years ago, I decided to release these audios to the public as an app – I did so long before it was ready, but I knew I had to get it out to the world. To succeed, you must simply do your best and move forward; the entrepreneurs who wait until their product is 'perfect' are never the ones who win. The Activations app took off and to date it's helped hundreds of thousands of people, which has been incredibly fulfilling for me. It's also helped me to realize many of my financial dreams – I'm now a self-made multimillionaire – and it's completely changed my life.

Evolving from Old Self to Future Self

Today, I truly believe that I'm living my Future Self life. Every day, I see the reality that I once pictured in my mind, and it's both thrilling and humbling. Of course, there are still moments when I feel the pull to strive for more, to reach even further beyond where I am today. But this drive isn't about dissatisfaction; it's about growth. I believe that we're meant to keep evolving, to continuously aim higher while savoring where we are in the present. It's a delicate balance, living fully in the now while remaining open to what's next, always pushing the boundaries of possibility.

My transformation from Old Self to Future Self occurred slowly, and then... all at once. At some point, the lines began to blur between visualizing and acting *as if* I was already my Future Self and genuinely living and experiencing the life I once dreamed of. It crept up on me gradually until, suddenly, I had to pinch myself every single day to remind myself that it was all real.

Today, my bank account reflects the figures I posted on the vision board I created when I was 18, but the car I once dreamed of is no longer a priority. As I've grown and evolved into my Future Self, I can see that it's exactly what I expected yet completely different. Things often feel the way I visualized they would, but my interests have changed. I've become less materialistic than I thought I'd be. I realize now that money only goes so far, and I've started to deeply consider my spirituality.

Before we move on, I want to make an important point. When I refer to the Future Self, I don't mean a version of you that exists only in the future. I'm not using this term to encourage forever seeking something outside the present moment. The truth is that you can live your future life right now! You can decide to be your best self in any given moment.

And as I'll show you in this book, you get into that mindset by fully embodying the energy of your future, acting *as if* you're already the person you want to become, and simply allowing yourself to be the ideal version of you, now. If the term Future Self doesn't resonate with you, feel free to use alternatives, such as Favorite Self, Best Self, New Self, Higher Self, or Ideal Self.

How do we know how far we are right now from becoming our Future Self? The answer is to honestly assess our current habits, thoughts, and actions. Are they moving us closer to the person we want to become, or are they keeping us stuck? The journey from Old Self to Future Self is about aligning more closely with your ideal self every day, using the insights and tools I'll share in this book to guide your transformation. So, let's now uncover and explore the limitless potential inside of you – your Future Self.

Two Steps to Your Transformation

The idea of evolving from your Old Self to your Future Self might seem overwhelming, but in fact the process is quite straightforward. After almost a decade of studying personal transformation, I've distilled it into a simple but profound two-step formula. If you follow these two steps as I've set them out, they will change your life.

Before we dive in, I encourage you to dream big and push boundaries! I want you to really challenge yourself, to open up to every possibility that could exist. Get uncomfortable. Feel the growth. Don't limit yourself. Remember, the direction of your life is entirely up to you. You can earn millions. You can enjoy radiant health. You can have a fairytale relationship. You can have a massive impact on the world. You can design and create your future. This is your opportunity to start living with depth and purpose.

Step 1: Clarity

This initial step is intended to help you gain total clarity about the person you aspire to become and the life you want to lead. We often find ourselves stuck in a rut simply because we're unsure what it is we truly want. And this uncertainty breeds inaction. Most people wander through life without direction, and they often don't realize their dreams because they never take the time to define what those dreams are. How can we possibly achieve that big, beautiful life if we're unclear about what it is we're striving for?

Gaining clarity isn't just about identifying what you want; it's about deeply reflecting on who you need to become to live the life you dream of. It's about creating a detailed, vivid vision of your Future Self – the version of you who has *already* achieved the milestones, embodied the lifestyle, and cultivated the essence of your deepest desires.

This step involves more than just daydreaming about the car, career, or partner you want; it's about truly understanding the qualities and attributes you must develop, the habits you must establish, and the mindset you must cultivate to get them. Knowing exactly who your Future Self is will serve as the foundation of your transformation, influencing every decision you make, every action you take, and every thought you allow yourself to think. Getting clear about the life you want, and *the version of you that has that life*, is the initial spark that lights the path toward becoming who you're meant to be.

In today's world, distractions are everywhere. Our phones buzz with countless notifications. Our screens bombard us with a constant stream of information. The demands of work, life, and technology pull us in a million different directions, and with all this noise, taking a moment to connect with ourselves and quietly reflect on our life seems difficult. We get so caught up in responding to the latest text, scrolling through Instagram, or binge-watching our favorite shows that we forget to pause and think deeply about what we really want.

This endless flow of distractions keeps us from setting clear goals, and pursuing them, too. Without taking the time to sit and think, how can we ever find clarity? I'll say it again: taking the time to pause and consider in detail what you want your dream life to look like is crucial for your future success. The rest of this chapter is all about getting you there. Before we jump into that, though, I want to briefly introduce you to the next step.

Step 2: Becoming

Once you have clarity about what your dream life looks like, then you must *become* the person who has that life. Quite frankly, the person you are today is incapable of achieving the expansive life you long for; therefore, you need to evolve into a version of you who *can* achieve it – your Future Self – and then align with that version *before* it becomes your reality. Step 2, Becoming, is essentially reverse engineering your Future Self transformation, making it happen faster. You'll start to embody the person you want to be, and as you do, you'll naturally adopt the self-image – the thoughts, beliefs, emotions, habits, and decision-making processes – required to sustain the energy of that person.

Many people struggle to maintain the behavior and actions necessary to reach their goals, and this is because they haven't yet transformed into the version of them who has achieved those goals. What they're doing doesn't align with the self-image of the person they aspire to be. You, however, need to 'become' your Future Self *before* the physical version has manifested. And you must morph into this new identity gradually, *before* you feel fully prepared, before everything in your life aligns perfectly, and even before you think you're ready.

The process of Becoming allows you to start breaking free from the resistance put up by your Old Self now, in this moment. Trusting the process of Becoming before you're ready is exactly what will get you there. In Part II of the book, we'll journey into the why and how of Becoming. But you need to do something first.

Create Your Future Self

You're now going to design a detailed, fully rounded vision of your ideal Future Self and the goals, dreams, and ambitions you want to achieve as that person. This exercise requires deep introspection combined with the use of two tools that will help align you with this vision: visualization and journaling.

Visualization is a simple psychological technique that involves forming vivid mental images of our desired future actions and outcomes. Creating detailed pictures in our mind of the person we want to become – our Future Self – and how that person thinks and behaves effectively tricks the brain into thinking we're already there. Journaling is simply writing down your thoughts, feelings, and reflections in a notebook to understand them more clearly: here, you'll use it to dig deep and get your visualization juices flowing. Together, visualization and journaling will help you to create your desired future and then motivate you to focus on, and work toward, your Future Self.

The Five Pillars of Your Future Self

You'll cultivate your Future Self identity by visualizing it and writing about it through the lens of five pillars, or aspects – mental, financial, physical, spiritual, and social. The more vividly you can picture these five pillars of your Future Self, the easier it will be for you to start behaving as if you already are that person (use the illustration overleaf as a visual reminder.) The writing prompts I've provided for each pillar are designed to help you uncover and record exactly what it is you want. It's important to go into as much detail as possible when responding to these prompts, as this will help you to bring your Future Self persona to life.

To begin, grab a pen and your journal or notebook and find a quiet place to sit where you won't be disturbed. Take a few deep breaths to help you relax. Then work your way through each pillar, reflecting on the questions I've posed and responding to the writing prompts in your journal/notebook; I recommend spending at least 10 minutes on each pillar.

It's crucial to try to visualize each pillar/aspect of your Future Self identity in as much detail as you can, and fully feel the emotions associated with what you're picturing. Repeat this exercise until you sense that your Future Self persona is complete (you'll know when that is because it will feel whole and resonate deeply within you.)

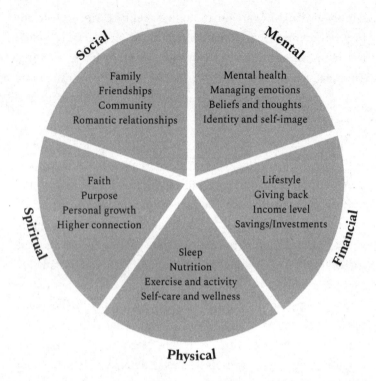

Social

Mental

Family
Friendships
Community
Romantic relationships

Mental health
Managing emotions
Beliefs and thoughts
Identity and self-image

Faith
Purpose
Personal growth
Higher connection

Lifestyle
Giving back
Income level
Savings/Investments

Spiritual

Financial

Sleep
Nutrition
Exercise and activity
Self-care and wellness

Physical

The Five Pillars of Your Future Self

Mental

How your Future Self perceives and interacts with the world will have a foundational impact on your life. Cultivating a strong and positive mindset and learning to speak to yourself in a constructive and helpful way will be crucial for maintaining everything you'll learn in this book. Adopting a set of empowering beliefs and carefully considering the types of thoughts you think every day will set you up to succeed; we'll talk more about changing your current thoughts, habits, and beliefs to more helpful and positive ones in Chapter 2.

What's the dominant mentality of your Future Self – is it an unshakable belief in your abilities, a self-empowering attitude ('I'm 100 percent responsible for my life!'), generally holding a positive outlook, or always believing you're in the right place at the right time and keeping the faith that everything happens for a reason? Get specific: Identify the core beliefs that drive your actions as your Future Self and the positive thoughts you have every day.

Picture how your Future Self views you and the environment around you. What are your beliefs about yourself and others? What's your baseline emotional state on a typical day? How do you react when things don't go to plan? To begin cultivating the mindset of your Future Self, reflect on these questions and then respond to the writing prompts below in your notebook or journal.

WRITING PROMPTS

+ Describe the mindset of my Future Self.

+ As my Future Self, how do I talk to myself? What type of thoughts do I have on a regular basis?

+ What core beliefs do I hold as my Future Self? How do these beliefs influence my behavior and decision-making?

+ How does my Future Self react to setbacks or unexpected challenges? What strategies do I use to regain composure and perspective?

+ Imagine a challenging situation and describe how my Future Self handles it.

✦ Describe a scenario in which my Future Self successfully shifts a negative mindset to a positive one. What steps do I take?

Financial

This key aspect of your life determines how your Future Self gets to live. Achieving financial stability is vital for living a life filled with freedom and joy. Additionally, feeling deeply fulfilled in your career will allow you to genuinely enjoy each day. Define what financial success looks like for you, whether it's earning a specific income, reaching a savings or investment goal, or being completely debt-free. Get specific: Understand exactly how much you want in savings, what your annual income should be, and how much of your income you plan to invest.

Visualize exactly how your Future Self manages, spends, and invests money. What do you spend your money on? What kind of home do you live in? Which career aligns with your Future Self lifestyle? Are you an entrepreneur, or do you work for a company? How much do you donate to charity each year? What do your bank accounts look like? Reflect on these questions and then respond to the writing prompts below to begin shaping a life that not only meets your financial needs but also brings you a deep level of personal satisfaction.

WRITING PROMPTS

✦ If I could have any level of income as my Future Self, which one would make me feel the most expanded and excited?

+ How much money would I like to have in savings and investments? What would my investment portfolio look like? Real estate, stocks, art?

+ What would I do with full financial freedom? What trips would I take? Which charitable organizations would I donate to? How much would I spend on self-care? Would I have a personal chef? Fly first class? What car would I own? What about the home(s) I'd live in?

+ Break down the amount my Future Self earns and spends in a month. For example, $20,000/month income: $5,000 on rent/mortgage; $2,000 on food and dining out; $1,000 on health and self-care; $500 to charity; $5,000 to investments and savings; $2,000 on travel and leisure; $1,500 on education or personal development; $2,000 on shopping; and $1,000 on miscellaneous or unexpected expenses.

+ What does a typical day in my ideal job look like? What are my tasks? Who do I interact with? How do I feel at the end of the working day?

+ What are the three major career milestones I want to achieve? Being on the *Forbes* 30 Under 30 list? Speaking on stage in front of 10,000 people? Being promoted to a C-suite role?

Physical

This aspect of your life shapes how your Future Self looks, feels, and moves. Achieving your health and fitness goals is one of those things that helps you live a life filled with energy and vitality. Being healthy makes you more radiant, more likely to live a longer life, and in every way enhances your existence. Let's get specific. Define what optimal health means for you, whether it's having a toned body, great posture, clear and glowing skin, healthy hair, or even being able to run a marathon!

Visualize your Future Self maintaining that good physique and health. What does your workout routine look like? What kinds of food do you eat, and what kinds do you limit? How does your body look and feel? Do you use the sauna or cold plunge? Go to the chiropractor weekly? Have annual health checks to ensure your nutrient levels are in the right place? Reflect on these questions to begin crafting a life that not only meets your physical health needs but also brings you a deep level of personal satisfaction and confidence.

WRITING PROMPTS

+ Describe the daily health and fitness routines of my Future Self.

+ What do I eat every day? What's my relationship like with food and working out?

+ Describe in detail what my Future Self's body looks like – my muscle tone, flexibility, posture, hair, and skin. How does it feel to move and exist in this body? How do I carry myself when I walk into a room?

+ Describe my personal style. What do I wear every day that feels aligned with my ultimate self? How do I present myself?

+ What are my core beliefs about health, wellness, and beauty? How have these beliefs shaped my approach to my daily habits?

+ Visualize my Future Self radiating with good health, beauty, and vitality, and exuding a vibrant energy that draws others in. How does it feel to embody a state of well-being that shines from the inside out?

Spiritual

Many people believe that to experience a true sense of meaning, purpose, and value in life, we must feel connected to something greater than ourselves. Practices that cultivate spirituality – such as following a religion, practicing mindfulness, journaling, connecting deeply with nature or art, or simply noticing life's synchronicities – can improve our health and emotional well-being and help us develop a positive mindset. Define what spirituality means to you and choose an approach that best nurtures your soul and empowers you to create the life you envision.

WRITING PROMPTS

+ Describe the spiritual practices or rituals my Future Self engages in regularly to cultivate inner peace and clarity. Do I journal? Pray? Read books about spirituality and personal development? Or maybe I perform acts of service to keep myself grounded and connected to others. How do these practices enhance my spiritual and emotional well-being?

+ Picture my Future Self experiencing a strong sense of connection to a higher power, to the present moment, to self, to others, to nature.

✦ Visualize moments of awe and wonder that awaken my sense of spirituality, whether it's standing at the base of a waterfall and feeling the mist land gently on my skin or encountering acts of kindness and compassion in the world around me.

✦ How do my spiritual beliefs influence the choices I make and the way I show up in the world? Do they align with my principles, such as compassion, integrity, and authenticity?

Remember that your inner spiritual life will evolve over time, so revisit this pillar once in a while to review what inspires and fuels your Future Self.

Social

Strong and healthy social connections are crucial for living a life rich in love, support, and community. Being socially connected enhances your emotional well-being, provides networks of support, and enriches every aspect of your existence.

Picture all the different ways that your Future Self connects, builds, and nurtures relationships with others. Define what a thriving social life means for your Future Self, whether it's having a close-knit circle of friends, a supportive family, engaging community ties, or meaningful romantic relationships. Get specific.

Visualize your Future Self cultivating and maintaining social connections. What does your social routine look like? How often do you engage with friends and family, and in what settings? How do you contribute to your relationships? What boundaries do you set in order to maintain healthy interactions? Do you participate in community service or social clubs? How do you handle conflicts or disagreements?

Reflect on these questions to begin crafting a life that not only meets your social needs but also brings you a profound level of personal fulfillment and joy.

WRITING PROMPTS

+ Describe my Future Self's weekly social activities. How do I balance time spent with my friends, family, and a romantic partner?

+ What qualities do I cherish in my friends, partners, family members? How do these relationships make me feel?

+ Describe a typical dinner party or other event hosted by my Future Self. What atmosphere do I create, and how do I make others feel welcome and valued?

+ How does my Future Self resolve conflicts or manage differences within relationships? What strategies do I use to ensure healthy and constructive communication?

+ Reflect on the quality of my social connections as my Future Self. Describe the characteristics of the people I surround myself with and how these relationships enrich my life.

+ Describe my communication style and how it's evolved over time. How do I express myself authentically and effectively, fostering open and honest communication in my relationships?

When your Future Self identity is complete, you'll find that there's nothing more to add; every element will feel right and align seamlessly with your deepest desires. This sense of completeness isn't just about establishing dreams and goals. It's about knowing that your Future Self is a true reflection of who you want to be; who you know, deep down, you're meant to be.

The goals you set and your responses to the writing prompts aren't set in stone. You can come back, adjust, and redefine them and your envisioned Future Self identity at any time. You have full permission to tweak it as needed – I do it often!

As they visualize their Future Self and their dream life as part of achieving clarity, some people conjure up highly specific aspects – the scent of the leather in their new Porsche, say, or the salty air at their beach home. And while thinking about it in this degree of detail can make our desired future life seem more attainable, what's truly crucial is how it *feels* to have reached that future life. In the next chapter, we're going to focus on that feeling. The visualization and writing exercise you've just completed is designed to help you gain clarity on the tangible aspects of your Future Self, but the real transformation occurs when you start *feeling* as if you already are that person.

CHAPTER 2

Be Your Future
Self Now

Now that you've created a fully fleshed vision of your ideal Future Self, it's essential to understand how it *feels*, in your body, to *be* that person right now, in the present moment. I cannot stress this strongly enough. You must teach your body to physically experience the thrill and passion tied to the potential of your envisioned life, or you'll never get there. As the great American writer and researcher Dr. Joe Dispenza says, 'Thoughts are the language of the brain, feelings are the language of the body.'[1]

If you close this book now and merely think about what you want without feeling it, your life won't change. Even if you imagine every last detail of it! You must feel your future life and the identity of your Future Self deeply and do so with your body more than your mind. This is where many manifestation experts miss the mark. It's not only *thinking* about what we want; it's about embodying, feeling, and being it, and a wealth of scientific data and studies reveals why.

Understanding the Biofield

Are you able to sense the energy that a person gives off, whether it feels positive or negative? Or has anyone ever told you that you have 'good energy'? These notions are not baseless, because science tells us that everything in the universe is made up of energy, and this energy vibrates at various frequencies. And today, there's growing interest in many different disciplines in the concept of energy and how it affects our daily lives.[2]

All living organisms, including humans, animals, and plants, are surrounded and permeated by interacting fields of energy, which scientists call the biofield. Dr. Joe Dispenza has been instrumental in helping us to understand the biofield and explain the quantum mechanics behind it. In his book *Becoming Supernatural* he describes the biofield as 'fields of energy and information' existing independently of space and time. You can't see them. But that doesn't mean they don't exist.[3]

According to practitioners of Reiki and other energy-based therapies, the human biofield is surprisingly large; it can radiate anywhere from about 6ft (2m) to 66ft (20m) from a person's body.[4] This may mean that whenever we're with other people, our biofields are intermingling. We're picking up signals from others' biofields all the time, as they are from us. We all utilize our biofield as a sensory tool – much like having an intuitive sixth sense.

The biofield may also have the power to guide our life in a specific direction, whether we're conscious of its existence or not; it may determine what we attract into our life on an energetic level, and this is why *feeling* is more important than *thinking*. Have you ever felt a tingle at the nape of your neck when someone's gaze was fixed on you from behind? Or had an affinity for certain people while feeling discomfort around others? Given that the biofield extends beyond the body, these inexplicable sensations could stem from your biofield detecting either harmonious or unpleasant energies within someone else's biofield.

As the writer and researcher Dawson Church says in his book *Mind to Matter*, 'When you change your mind, sending new signals through the neural pathways of your brain, altering the energy fields all around you, interacting with the fields of others, you have no idea how far the effect might travel.'[5]

You Are Magnetic

Still not convinced that the biofield exists? Let's look at how scientists have detected it in both humans and plants. In 1963, Gerhard Baule and Richard McFee from Syracuse University in the US used magnetic coils and a sensitive amplifier to measure the magnetic field (biofield) that's projected by the human heart; and in 1972, following the introduction of an ultra-sensitive instrument called a magnetometer, David Cohen of MIT was able to record the magnetic field around a person's head produced by brain activities.[6]

More recent research by the HeartMath Institute in the US reveals that the heart's magnetic field can be detected several feet away from the body, in all directions, using magnetometers. It's also been discovered that all tissues and organs in the human body produce specific magnetic pulsations and that mapping the body's biofield often gives a more accurate indication of a person's health and wellness than traditional electrical measurements.[7]

Further compelling evidence of the human biofield is the phenomenon of phantom limb syndrome. Many amputees report feeling sensations, such as pain or itching, in limbs that have been removed. Is it possible that the missing limb might still exist within the biofield?[8]

Kirlian photography is another interesting technique for detecting the biofield. When an object is placed on a photographic plate in a high-voltage, high-frequency electrical field and photographed using a specially developed camera, the resulting Kirlian photographs reveal glowing, colorful balls of light around the object, which are its energy level or biofield.

The phantom leaf effect is a mind-blowing phenomenon that lets us peek into the biofield of plants. In experiments where up to 50 percent of a leaf was cut away and the leaf was photographed using a Kirlian camera, the entire structure, including the absent portion, still appeared in the image. And the image was so detailed that the spine, veins, and skin of the missing part of the leaf were visible. The phantom leaf effect occurs because plants have a system of vascular bundles that transport water, nutrients, and sugars. When part of a leaf is removed, these bundles seal off to prevent leakage, yet the leaf's shape often leaves an imprint on the plant.[9] It's similar to pressing your hand into soft clay and seeing the impression left behind. The phantom leaf effect and Kirlian photography offer incredible visual insights into these invisible forces that sustain life.

Step into Your Future Self Energy

So, what does all this have to do with creating your Future Self? A lot! There's an entire narrative unfolding alongside us that we don't ever pay attention to (or see), and it has a significant effect on our life and well-being.

Scientific research confirms that our heart's rhythmic beating patterns not only reflect our emotional state but also play a direct role in determining our emotional experience.[10] The heart's magnetic field, which we discussed earlier, forms a complex energetic network that connects with the magnetic fields throughout the rest of the body.

In essence, the heart acts as the conductor from which all systems flow. When we feel better emotionally, we naturally feel better physically. This alignment allows us to create better outcomes in our lives. As this momentum builds, it generates a continuous flow of health at the biofield level, physical level, and emotional level, making it easier to embody and live in our Future Self energy *now*.

The human biofield influences matter and the life we live, and with intention, we have the power to adjust the 'energetic set point' at which it is maintained and create what I call a Future Self frequency, which will help us attract and become everything we've ever wanted. By creating and embodying your Future Self frequency, you can align your biofield, your emotional state, and your physical health to manifest your ideal life more effectively. And the process is simple. In fact, it's fascinating how straightforward it is to understand this frequency and become familiar with the *feeling* of embodying it.

Each person's Future Self frequency is unique to them because the feelings we associate with the things we desire are based on our personal views and experiences. Your Future Self frequency encapsulates everything that you want in your future. It's the sensation of actually living as your Future Self. It's a single, expansive, and unlimited feeling.

Discover Your Future Self Frequency

To discover your Future Self frequency, you must first identify the top three to five positive emotions that you associate with the Future Self persona you created in Chapter 1. Then take a minute to intensely visualize and feel these feelings *together* in your body. Here's a detailed guide to this process, followed by a quick exercise to reinforce it.

There are numerous positive emotions, but the ones that people use most often to describe how they feel when they are most aligned with their Future Self are joy, love, bliss, gratitude, abundance, wealth, pride, peace, vitality, awe, confidence, health, happiness, fulfillment. However, it's about which words resonate the most with you emotionally and trigger the right feelings.

Begin with one of these emotions. Let's use *love* as an example. Feel that love inside and around your body, then introduce the next emotion while maintaining that foundational feeling of love. Perhaps the next one is *health*. Explore what it feels like in your body to feel love – a heart-centered, expansive, beautiful sensation – and then add the feeling of health, which includes the sensations of vitality and energy. Play with that for a moment. As you do this, continue to feel the love in your heart. Feel it inside and around you. Then layer in the feeling of health while keeping the love present.

When you're able to hold both love and health simultaneously, introduce your third emotion; in this example we'll use *wealth*. Maintain the feelings of love and health, and then add the feeling of wealth – perhaps this feels expansive, unlimited, and full of opportunity. Now, merge that feeling of wealth with love and health, maintaining the strong energies in all three, at the same time, feeling the unique frequency of combining them.

Most people find fulfillment with three to five positive emotions because each one, like love and health, casts a wide net. Love might include loving yourself and being in a loving relationship with a romantic partner. Health might involve having a certain muscle tone and waking up every morning with vital energy.

My current personal Future Self frequency is the combination of love, abundance, awe, and health. For my best life, love is the driver of it all. I think about the people I love, how I love myself, and how in love I am with life! Abundance, to me, means wealth in many areas; it's about having an abundance of everything I desire: money, opportunities, joy, bliss, without limits. Awe, to me, is about seeing the magic in the world; it keeps my life exciting and full of surprises from the universe that give me goosebumps. For me, health is feeling strong, lean, and full of energy and focus. This combination, this frequency, shapes what it feels like to be my Future Self, and it's always evolving.

What Does Your Frequency Feel Like?

I want you to really understand what your Future Self frequency feels like inside of you. In your notebook or journal, write down the three to five emotions that make up *your* Future Self frequency. Then close your eyes and complete these three steps:

1. Focus on the first emotion and visualize it with your body. How does it feel to fully live in this emotion?

2. Once you've fully embodied this first emotion, bring in the second one. Ensure that you're not losing the full-body feeling of the first emotion, simply adding to it, mixing it together with the second one until they have combined equally in your body.

3. Follow the same steps for the remaining emotions on your list, combining them into one, supercharged feeling – *this* is your Future Self frequency.

Don't continue reading until you've done this and created your Future Self frequency, okay? It's very important. It will set you up to get the most out of the rest of this book and form the foundation of your future life. How much do you want to live this big, beautiful future life? Your energy creates your life. The Future Self persona you've created for yourself creates your life.

Now that you've defined your Future Self frequency, memorize it. Feel it in your body and begin living with this frequency as your baseline. Envision yourself stepping into this Future Self life right now – adopting the habits, mannerisms, and mindset that align with this version of you. Knowing your Future Self frequency and learning to embody it will make your transformation easier and give you something to revert to when you stop feeling like your best self. It's the fastest way to change old patterns and make new decisions aligned with your Future Self.

Feel What You Desire in Your Body

As I explained earlier, while you're connecting with your Future Self, you must make sure to feel and see that person with your body not just with your mind. It's easy to think things, but when you feel things deeply, you imprint these feelings into your body and your biofield. This makes your visualizations far more powerful and effective.

When you feel positive emotions deeply, you enhance your ability to manifest the life you want. The positive emotions associated with your desires – when felt deeply in your body, especially in your heart – emit an electromagnetic signature into your biofield and environment. This transforms you into a powerful magnet for your desires.

On the contrary, when you experience negative emotions deeply, you attract more of that negativity into your life. Have you ever noticed that a bad day only gets worse? You might start out feeling annoyed or negative, and then, seemingly in sync, your hot coffee spills over you during your drive to work, or your shirt gets hooked on a doorknob, causing you to stumble. This only happens when you're already having a bad day, doesn't it? It's the same principle: You're always attracting circumstances into your life, whether you realize it or not.

When you *feel* what you desire in your body, you become more magnetic toward it. So, while you're visualizing and embodying your Future Self, make sure that you're deeply feeling it in your body. Notice the sensations of love in your chest, the goosebumps of excitement on your arms, the feeling of abundance in your biofield. This is how you attract your desires faster and more effortlessly: by *feeling* them deeply.

Feel It Before You Have It

Imagine that today, out of nowhere, you land a dream opportunity. Maybe it's an incredible new job with an annual salary of $300,000, or a surprise prize worth a million dollars.

This opportunity is going to change your life forever. There's then a short delay before you receive it – if it's your dream job, say, it might take a week or two for you to start it and get that first paycheck – but during that time your energy is completely different. You're walking, moving, and holding yourself differently because you know that this is now your reality. You're wealthy, and you have the potential to travel the world and do whatever you dream of.

> *The trick to connecting with and activating*
> *your Future Self is embodying the energy of*
> *your future before it actually happens.*

You need to have that deep expectation, that inner knowing, that this is who you are, and this is your life.

People often ask me, 'How do I act as if I'm already a wealthy future version of myself when I don't have the money yet?' I tell them, act like you know it's coming. Feel it as if it's already there because that's the essence of who you are. How do you feel in the days before that big new paycheck clears? Bubbling excitement, a sense of abundance? That's the feeling you need to align with. *That's* your Future Self frequency.

CASE STUDY: ALLIE

Here's a real-life example of the Feel It Before You Have It principle in action. Allie had always dreamed of living a life of abundance, but for years, she struggled with feelings of scarcity and self-doubt. A middle school teacher with a modest income, she often worried about paying bills and never felt truly secure in her financial situation.

Allie had tried visualization techniques and was aware of Activations, but it wasn't until she truly embraced the Feel It Before You Have It principle that her life began to change. After learning about how powerful it is to feel her desires in her body, Allie committed to embodying the frequency of wealth. She'd spend time each morning visualizing her Future Self as financially free, feeling the excitement of having money flow effortlessly into her life. But instead of just picturing the money, she tapped into the feeling of abundance. She imagined the joy of being able to pay for vacations without stress, the peace of having savings in the bank, and the thrill of walking into her favorite store and buying items without checking the price tags.

Allie practiced this every day. As she went about her regular routine, she'd consciously walk as if she already had the financial freedom she desired. She noticed how her posture changed, how she smiled more, and how much more confident she felt. The emotions of excitement and gratitude started to feel real in her body, even though her bank account hadn't changed – yet.

Just a few months into her new practice, opportunities began to appear. A former student, now a successful entrepreneur, reached out to Allie with an offer to collaborate on an educational consulting project that would pay double her teaching salary. Soon after, Allie received an unexpected inheritance from a distant relative, which allowed her to invest in real estate. Within a year, Allie was making more money than she'd ever imagined, living the abundant life she once thought was out of reach. Looking back, she believes the shift happened not because she worked harder or got lucky but because she changed her energy. She felt wealthy *before* the money came, and her life followed suit.

The Magic of Activations

In Chapter 1, I told you how I developed a new type of audio called Activations, but I'd like to go deeper in explaining what these are and how, along with the other tools and strategies in the book, they can help you to feel that you are already your Future Self.

There's a time and place for relaxation techniques and meditation, and I'm not devaluing those practices, but thinking that they are the key to actively transforming your confidence, relationships, and bank account is simply incorrect. My goal for you is to unlock real and lasting change in as little time as possible, and I believe that Activations are one of the best shortcut tools you can use to get there. With their potent mix of visualization techniques, emotive music, and motivational guidance, Activations raise our energy and inspire and motivate us to connect deeply with our Future Self.

You can play Activations in the background as you go about your daily life, just as you do with podcasts, music, or audiobooks. The unique benefit of listening to Activations is that they guide you to develop positive and empowering new beliefs and thoughts, even *while* you're engaged in everyday activities like cooking, walking, getting dressed, driving to work, or putting on makeup. This helps ensure that you're constantly aligned with the energy of your Future Self, making every step forward feel inevitable. Learning to be your Future Self in everyday moments is more powerful than anything else you can do, and Activations are an easy way to habit stack.

Like all the visualization tools in this book, listening to Activations goes beyond simply imagining change – in time, it will rewire your brain, making genuine transformation a reality. And, unlike a meditation practice, it doesn't require you to carve out time in your day. It's difficult for me to describe in words what it feels like to use Activations. You really need to try it yourself. I'm very confident that you'll experience an immediate shift in your energy if you do, so I'm giving readers an exclusive offer to try the Activations app for 90 days completely free; head to www.activations.com/book or scan the QR code below.

Create Your Own Activations

We have a growing library of more than 700 Activations on the app, but if you'd rather create your own personalized version of an Activation to play while you're using the book to connect with your Future Self, let me show you two simple ways to do this.

Version 1: Using an audio recording app (such as Voice Memos on iPhone), record yourself as you speak for between five and 20 minutes about your ideal future and the person you aspire to be. Describe in detail how it feels to live the life you desire. Include affirmations and motivational phrases, such as:

- I feel so much fulfillment in my life now that I've reached x milestone.

- I am exactly where I need to be, and I feel so much peace knowing that everything I desire is in the process of unfolding.

- I feel so light and strong now that I've prioritized my health – it feels so good to feel good!

Ensure that the tone of your voice is confident, upbeat, and inspiring. The goal is to infuse your words with the energy of your Future Self, so that when you listen to your Activation as you go about your day, you can feel that frequency throughout your body.

Version 2: For a more immersive experience, play music in the background while you record your Activation; this will amplify the effects of your visualization, affirmations, and description of your ideal life. Choose energizing and uplifting music that feels like a powerful 'movie moment' – perhaps one of the frequencies I've recommended on pages 36–37.

At the end of each part of this book, you'll find an Activation script which encapsulates the themes of Clarity, Becoming, and Maintaining; you can record yourself reading this script, too, using either of the methods above, or listen to it on the Activations app.

Once you've recorded your Activation, whether it's with or without background music, you'll notice how powerful sound can be in shifting your energy. Let's explore how listening to the right music can further elevate your state and deepen your connection with your Future Self.

Using Music to Change Your State

You know that feeling you get when you listen to a particularly intense and beautiful part of a song? Perhaps it's the exciting chorus that makes you feel so many emotions, all at once. Or the verse that floods you with hope, clarity, and a deep romanticism for life. Or that 'main character' verse, where you feel like you're the lead in a movie, and your state is elevated. Music has the power to make us feel a specific way and the water experiment conducted by the Japanese author Masaru Emoto may reveal why.

In his book *The Hidden Messages in Water*, Emoto asserted that different emotional stimuli, such as positive or negative thoughts, words, or music, influences the molecular structure of water.[11] As part of his research, he played positive and negative music to water and then froze the water and examined the ice crystals under a microscope.

As a baseline, the water that wasn't exposed to any music formed simple, plain hexagonal crystals. However, when Beethoven's 'Pastoral Symphony' was played to the water, the crystals transformed into complex, delicate patterns. John Lennon's 'Imagine' inspired the water to form flower-like crystals, while J.S. Bach's compositions resulted in stunning, intricate designs. In contrast, when the water was exposed to heavy metal music, it failed to form crystals and instead became coarse and irregular.

Given that half of the human body is made up of water, these findings may show that the music we listen to influences our physical and emotional states. Harmonious, positive music may create a state of balance and health, while negative, dissonant music could lead to disorder and stress within our bodies. This potential connection highlights the importance of choosing the right music to listen to, not only for our health but also for the state we must be in to transform into our Future Self.

Music That Aligns You with Your Future Self

Now, I haven't yet talked about the powerful effect that our words, thoughts, and emotions have on our bodies – I cover this in depth in Chapter 4. However, I wanted to make the point here that while you're creating and learning to become your Future Self, you should only listen to music that makes your energy positive and elevated. I highly recommend listening to the frequencies listed below throughout your day – they can influence your chemical makeup in a matter of moments. Search for them online; they are available for free on YouTube or Spotify. These are also the frequencies we use in the Activations app.

417 Hz: Clearing Negativity

This frequency is known for its ability to clear away negative energy and emotional blockages. It helps us break old patterns and beliefs, making space for positive thoughts and energy, thus preparing our mind for manifestation.

432 Hz: The Miracle Tone

This frequency is associated with deep healing and emotional well-being. It's believed to resonate harmoniously with the Earth's natural frequency, promoting relaxation, reducing stress, and enhancing overall health.

528 Hz: Love and Transformation

528 Hz is associated with DNA repair and transformation. It promotes the manifestation of a better life, from more abundance to more love and joy. This frequency is also linked to a reduction in stress and anxiety, fostering inner peace and deep positivity.

639 Hz: Harmonizing Relationships

This frequency is connected with the heart and is known for promoting harmony in relationships. It enhances communication, understanding, and love, making it ideal for attracting positive relationships and healing emotional traumas.

741 Hz: Activating Mental Clarity

The 741 Hz frequency is associated with problem-solving and awakening intuition. It helps clear emotional blockages and promotes mental clarity, making it easier to find solutions and achieve your goals.

963 Hz: Activating Future Self Consciousness

Referred to as the 'Frequency of the Gods,' 963 Hz is associated with spiritual enlightenment. It helps restore a sense of unity with the universe and promotes deep inner peace and connection with your Future Self.

Old Self Beliefs vs. Future Self Beliefs

A key part of achieving clarity is recognizing the beliefs held by your Old Self and reprogramming them to align with the truths you want to embrace from this moment onward. Not tomorrow, not next week, but today – right now. Once you identify what you want to be true, you must transform in that moment.

Open your journal or notebook – it's time to compare and contrast your Old Self beliefs with your ideal Future Self beliefs. Draw a line down the middle of a new page. On the left, write down your Old Self beliefs. On the right, list the new beliefs that align with your Future Self. Write down as many beliefs as you can and take as much time as needed until you feel completely satisfied that you've covered everything. Here are some examples to get you started:

Old Self Beliefs

- I'm a victim of circumstances.

- I hold no power over my future.

- The things that happen are out of my control.

- I'm not good enough.

- I'll be happy when...

Future Self Beliefs

- I am 100 percent responsible for my life.

- I create my reality.

- My reaction to the things that happen is what matters.

- I love myself just the way I am.

- I'm happy now while striving for more.

This is your accountability exercise. Just do it. Many people have the desire to change but never get started. This and the other exercises in this part of the book are that crucial first step. Whether you complete them or not will be a determining factor in your success. Acting now will set the foundation for embodying your Future Self and creating the life you desire.

Remember, you're negotiating this power dynamic with yourself. No one can get in the way of this energy exchange but you. Accept responsibility and empower your Future Self, who is sending you love and encouragement in every moment. Cut through the chaos and negative mental chatter and pay attention to them.

Snapping Out of Numbness

If you've been following all the suggestions in Part I but are still feeling unsure about creating your Future Self and identifying your goals, the reason might be more obvious than you think: you're numb. If you're filling your days with activities, foods, and substances that numb your body and mind and disconnect you from your true self – such as mindless scrolling on social media, constant distractions, an overwhelming workload, alcohol, drugs, overeating, a poor diet, or excessive TV watching or gaming – you cannot gain clarity about your future.

You're trying to connect with your deepest desires while being bombarded by things that dull your senses, so it's no wonder you feel stuck. You might think that these things help you to unwind, but in fact they only add layers to the confusion and cloud your ability to get clear on what you want. However, it's crucial to understand that a significant wake-up call can spark immediate clarity. Consider those who, even in the throes of addiction, have had a moment of profound realization that catalyzed a drastic life change. While snapping out of numbness is challenging, it's possible.

If you don't yet feel sufficiently clear-minded to create your Future Self, try eliminating the sources of numbness outlined above for a week and allow yourself to sit with your thoughts, free from distractions. Consider cutting out gluten and sugar as well – these dietary changes can make you feel incredibly clear. Or try a 24-hour fast to reset your body and mind. By cleansing your system of mental and physical junk, you'll likely find that clarity emerges quickly.

Then revisit the exercises 'Create Your Future Self' on page 10 and 'Discover your Future Self Frequency' on page 26. If a full week seems daunting and you haven't yet completed these exercises, try isolating yourself for a chunk of time – a day, an evening, or a morning. Put your phone and other technology in another room, turn them off, and commit to staying in that space until you achieve clarity.

From Numbness to Aliveness

We're often our own worst enemy, making countless excuses to avoid doing the work. So, break free from numbness, take responsibility for your life, and keep pushing forward. Partaking in numbing activities dulls not only your senses but also your spirit. It prevents you from accessing the vibrant, creative, and intuitive parts of yourself that are essential for genuine clarity.

Clarity requires a clear channel, free from the static of daily life. When you strip away the distractions we've just discussed, you allow your true thoughts and feelings to surface. This detoxification process can be uncomfortable at first; you might feel restless, anxious, or even bored. But as you persist, you'll find that your mind begins to settle, and your thoughts become more focused. Without the constant influx of external stimuli, your mind can finally align with your true north. This is where real clarity comes from – a deep understanding of what you want and where you're going.

Imagine for a moment that you've decided to cut out all distractions for a week. You've stopped drinking, set aside your phone, and committed to eating clean. The first day might be tough. You may have withdrawal symptoms – not just from substances like caffeine or sugar, but simply reaching for your phone. But by the second or third day, something magical starts to happen. Your thoughts become clearer. You start to notice things about yourself that were previously buried under layers of distraction.

This newfound clarity can lead to profound insights. You might discover that some of the goals you thought were important to you are in fact reflections of societal expectations or the influence of others. Without the numbing effects of daily distractions, you can finally hear your own inner voice clearly. This is your highest Future Self voice. You might find yourself reevaluating your relationships, your habits, and your overall lifestyle, too. This is a natural and necessary part of the process. Embrace it. Allow yourself to make changes based on these insights. This is how you move from confusion and numbness to clarity.

> *This journey to becoming your Future Self is about more than just achieving goals. It's about becoming the most vibrant, authentic version of yourself.*

When you strip away the layers of numbness, you reconnect with your true essence. This is where true power and fulfillment lies – in the ability to create a life that's genuinely fulfilling and aligned with your deepest desires and truest self.

So, take that step. Cleanse yourself of the distractions and decisions that are holding you back. And when you return to the visualization and journaling exercises we looked at earlier, you'll do so with a clear mind and a focused heart, ready to define and pursue your true path.

You Want What You Want for a Reason

Imagine that your Future Self is guiding your every decision and actively shaping your desires for you. Although this sounds like science fiction, it may well be the truth when viewed through the lens of the transactional interpretation of quantum mechanics, a groundbreaking theory developed by John G. Cramer, a renowned physicist at the University of Washington.[12]

In highly simplified terms, the transactional interpretation explains how particles send out waves forward and backward in time, creating a quantum 'handshake' between the present and the future. We can think of it like a conversation between different points in time, where our Old Self can communicate with our Future Self.

Cramer's theory implies that your thoughts and actions today may be influenced by events that are yet to happen or even your Future Self trying to communicate with you. Your desires aren't random. Those gut instincts that you have, that inexplicable certainty about a path you need to take – you have these feelings because you're being led toward a certain path by forces greater than you. This is your Future Self, your ultimate potential lifeline, sending signals to guide you.

Trust that your Future Self is guiding you and that your desires are meaningful and intentional.

To some, this may be a speculative idea, but I believe it's a logical interpretation of Cramer's theory, which indicates that the boundaries of time are more fluid than we ever imagined. Reaching this understanding revolutionized the way I view my own desires. Now when I feel drawn to a specific experience or goal, I believe it's because my Future Self knows that achieving it will bring me fulfillment and growth. Nothing in the universe is random – every event, every desire, has a purpose and this truth underlines the interconnectedness of our past, present, and future selves.

Embracing this idea can transform your life. You'll begin to feel divinely led and start seeing the magic of being alive *everywhere*. Your dreams and aspirations really mean something; they are powerful guided feelings from your future potential, urging you to become the person you're meant to be.

Moving Forward Not Backward

Our brains are hardwired for survival, and this programming drives us to seek safety and consistency, making us lean toward the familiar – even when it's not what's best for us. Our Old Self, with all its flaws, often feels safer than stepping into the unknown. This comforting familiarity is a powerful primal force, pulling us back to our Old Self behaviors and beliefs rather than propelling us forward into our abundant Future Self life.

This tendency to revert to the Old Self isn't just about comfort. It's about clarity too. We know our present selves intimately; we've spent years in that persona, understanding our desires, fears, and behaviors. This self actually feels like us. In contrast, at the start of our transformation journey, our vision of our Future Self can be blurry – an amalgamation of aspirations and qualities that it seems difficult to form into a clear picture. It can be muddled, with conflicting goals or disjointed qualities that don't quite add up to a coherent identity, or a unified Future Self persona.

Even when our past experiences weren't positive, they don't hold the uncertainty of the future. There's a paradoxical comfort in the familiar pain, whereas the future, rich with unknowns and possibilities, can often evoke fear and anxiety. Our comfort zones are shaped by our past experiences, and this particular comfort zone can become an invisible boundary – subtly discouraging us from pushing beyond the Old Self. Stepping into the unknown requires energy and risk, whereas living as the Old Self offers a path of least resistance.

Feeling safe in our comfort zones is an unconscious evolutionary survival strategy that's deeply embedded in our biology. Our ancestors' survival often depended on their adherence to known, safe environments where the variables were controlled, and the risks were minimal. Venturing into unknown territories could mean encountering predators, hostile environments, or scarce resources. Naturally, our brains evolved to prefer safety and predictability, gravitating toward repeating past behaviors and staying within the confines of familiar settings.[13]

Being aware of this aspect of human psychology is the first step in overcoming it. We need to make our Future Self as real and detailed as our Old Self. This means that when we envision our Future Self and our dream life we must do so with as much specificity and emotional connection as we can muster.

The more vivid and tangible our picture of our future, the more compelling it becomes.

Recognizing this pull is the first step; then we can actively work to stretch our boundaries and redefine our comfort zones. So, while our brains might be wired to look back, we have the power to rewire them to look forward. By repeatedly visualizing our desired future, engaging with it in thought, emotion, and action, we begin to make the unknown known. We transform, little by little, every single time we embody our Future Self frequency. We get closer to living our desired Future Self life every single time we choose to change, and the tools in this book have been designed to make this change from the unknown both effortless and enjoyable.

ACTIVATION:
GET CLARITY ON YOUR FUTURE SELF

Your Future Self is the version of you that lives the life you desire.

This version of you has the relationships you desire, the success you desire, the health you desire, the happiness you desire.

By designing your ideal Future Self, you're opening yourself up to the exponential growth that only finding clarity can create.

And with clarity, you will begin to experience the life you were meant to live.

So right now, decide:

How does your Future Self live?

What kind of life do you want to create?

To transform, you must first get crystal clear about who you want to be – the best possible version of you.

What do they have?

What kind of life do they live?

How do they feel about themselves?

Begin to visualize this Future Self version of you, leading with desire – those deep wants inside of your soul.

Tuning in to your intuition, a deep knowing that these things, this life, is meant for you.

Keep visualizing your Future Self, seeing a clear picture of who they are and how it feels to be them.

What kind of life does your Future Self live?

Now is the time for you to choose who you want to be, for you to select your future reality.

It is time for you to finally change your old self-image.

Let this be the moment you choose your future, instead of passively letting life happen to you.

If anything was possible, what kind of life would you want?
If anything was possible, who would you become?

Remember to feel the energy of this Future Self version of you.
Begin creating a new feeling in your body, elevating your energy to match this higher frequency.
Feel what it feels like to be your Future Self now, to have all of your dreams come true.

As you feel your Future Self frequency, get super clear on what it's like to live in this state of being.
Feel that Future Self frequency inside and around you, like your body is in a bubble of this frequency.
Feel this elevated frequency running through your veins.
Become more this energy than anything else.

Let it consume you, let it take over your physical body.
This is the life you are meant to live.
And just know that you are exactly where you need to be in this moment to create this Future Self life of yours.
You deserve to live a life beyond your wildest dreams.

And this Future Self reality is closer than you think.

✦

You can use this script to create an Activation (*see instructions on pages 33–34*) or find it on the Activations app under Anytime Activations.

PART II

BECOMING

Welcome to Becoming, the second step in your Future Self transformation. Now that you've gained clarity on what you want and have envisioned the person you aspire to be, it's time to bring that vision to life.

In this section, you'll take the steps needed to consistently embody your Future Self, creating a continuous loop of growth and success. Who you become will be shaped by your ability to mold your identity. By making positive changes in three key areas – your thoughts, beliefs, and feelings; your environment; and your decisions – you'll build a cohesive self-image that aligns with the goals of your Future Self. This will lay the foundation for everything that follows, bridging the gap between who you are now and who you want to be.

If you commit to everything outlined in this section, you'll see your progress accelerate and your life begin to transform.

CHAPTER 3

Change Your Self-Image, Change Your Life

Your self-image is your perception of yourself, and how you appear to other people, including your physical appearance, personality, and characteristics. Developing over time, your self-image is influenced by factors such as culture, family, friends, and personal experiences, and it has a profound influence on your beliefs, your emotions, your behavior, and your relationships. Your self-image is the energy that you radiate out into the world, and it affects every aspect of your life. You cannot evolve into your Future Self without changing your self-image.

Your self-image, the way in which you view and evaluate yourself, whether it's positive or negative, and the expectations you hold are the reasons why you are where you are today. Your self-image affects the way you act, think, decide, speak, feel – all of it. The words you choose to put at the end of the sentence 'I'm the kind of person who...' will quite simply determine the trajectory of your life.

At the heart of every action, thought, and habit lies a deeply rooted self-image. But your self-image isn't fixed. It can be changed, and you have the power to change it. This chapter unravels the transformative power of understanding and then reshaping our self-image.

You're Not Who You Think You Are

The person that you supposedly are, right now, can morph into a completely different one with opposite characteristics. We believe that we're born as a specific type of person, and after decades of conditioning, conforming, and consistent behavior, we subconsciously 'play' this character. But in reality, we can change who we are simply by *deciding* to.

You can make the decision to alter your habits, your actions, and your responses. You can choose to become the person you dream of being. Are you socially awkward? A bit overweight? In debt? Not as confident as you'd like to be? You can change this.

Choose to be someone who thrives socially.

Decide to be fit and healthy.

Choose to create new income streams and manage your finances better.

Decide to be confident and charismatic.

Changing how you see yourself, your self-image, requires practice and dedication. The truth is that you have superhuman powers inside of you that you've barely tapped into yet. These powers enable you to do absolutely anything you can imagine. You might believe that you're locked into behaving in a certain way, but your personality can change just as easily as your body can change when you start eating better and working out. Your self, who you are, can transform in a short period of time if you embed new habits and thinking patterns into your daily routines. As I'll show you in the coming chapters, gaining control over your own brain is the secret to crafting an unbelievably exceptional life.

The way we perceive or think of ourselves, our self-image, determines how we act and what we achieve in every area of our lives; this is why it's so important to hold yourself in high regard, to have high self-esteem. When you like yourself, you'll make decisions that honor your whole being: body, mind, soul. We're designed to survive and thrive, and therefore we should pay attention to the inner instructions that our higher self gives us.

Addressing a Negative Self-Image

This is the natural flow of our inner divine system at work. We must learn to trust the creative force of our soul. Every word we say and every thought we have is powerful. When we negate our power through acts of self-sabotage and holding a negative self-image, we forfeit that power and lose both time and energy that should be focused on the present moment and activating our Future Self.

Consider confidence as an example of how a positive or negative self-image shapes our behavior. If you believe that you're confident and articulate, you'll act confidently and speak fluently. On the other hand, if you believe you're shy and terrible at socializing, that's simply how you'll behave. Eight years ago, I didn't know what being truly confident was. Social interaction made me feel nervous. I was the quintessential people-pleaser, hoping to be liked, and I'd practically black out from anxiety if I had to speak in front of a large group of people. My self-image was rooted in doubt and fear, which affected every social interaction I had.

Fast-forward to today and I'm now one of the most sociable and confident people I know. The transformation is profound. I can strike up a conversation with anyone with complete ease and grace. The anxiety that I once felt in every social setting is a distant memory. This newfound confidence has reshaped my daily life and opened countless doors and opportunities. And it all began with a pivotal shift in the way I viewed myself. Confidence isn't a trait; it's a skill. By changing my self-image and repeatedly *practicing* being a confident person, I've been able to step into a version of myself I once thought was unreachable.

The same goes with becoming a fit and healthy person. If you don't view yourself as someone who works out, establishing a routine of hitting the gym three or four times a week will seem daunting. However, if you deeply appreciate your health and you enjoy optimizing your body to feel and look its best, you'll naturally be inclined to cook healthy meals for yourself, limit alcohol, avoid late-night partying, and forgo other self-sabotaging lifestyle choices.

When you value looking and feeling healthy and see yourself as a person who lives a healthy lifestyle, this self-image will guide your daily actions. If you ever stray from this image – perhaps slipping back into old bad habits – you'll feel a strong pull to return to what feels right. This inner compass keeps you aligned with your vision of health, urging you to return to activities and choices that support your well-being. Identifying as a healthy person makes consistently doing healthy habits easy and it also makes it uncomfortable to deviate from them for too long.

Here's another example: If you've decided that you aren't 'a morning person,' guess what will inevitably happen? You'll dislike mornings. It will be difficult for you to wake up early because every single ounce of your being has been imprinted with this belief. This law applies to every and any belief we have about ourselves, such as:

- I'll never be successful because I wasn't born into money.

- I don't have time. I'm too busy.

- I'm not good enough to do that.

- There's no chance they'll say yes.

- I'm not special.

- I've never been good with money.

- It's too late to start investing.

- I don't have enough experience to do that.

- I'm too old/too young.

- I'm just an unlucky person.

- I've always been disorganized.

- I'm not creative.

- I'm always late.

- I don't like healthy foods.

- It's so hard to lose weight.

- I hate exercising.

- They're out of my league.

- I'm too quiet to meet new people.

- I'm an all-or-nothing person: I've never been good at balance.

- I could never give up alcohol.

- It's my one vice.

- This is just the way I am.

You're building your future experiences with the thoughts you think and the beliefs you believe, whether you like it or not.

*Every thought and belief you hold is
actively creating your future.*

Your beliefs were likely adopted throughout your childhood. Until the age of eight, our brains are like sponges soaking up information. This means that everything we were exposed to by our parents, friends, teachers, family, acquaintances, and the media imprinted heavily into our subconscious in the formative years of our life.

That being said, it doesn't matter where these beliefs came from. You could spend years trying to pinpoint the origins of this negative programming in order to put the blame on someone or something. Save yourself some time and decide to focus on your exciting future. All that matters now is that you actively change your negative Old Self beliefs and take your future into your own hands. We'll talk more about beliefs in the next chapter.

Go Straight to the Source

Imagine your self-image as the core of an onion, with every layer beyond it – your thought patterns, your beliefs and values, your emotions and feelings, your habits, and your relationships – being shaped and influenced by that core self-image; the illustration below depicts this concept.

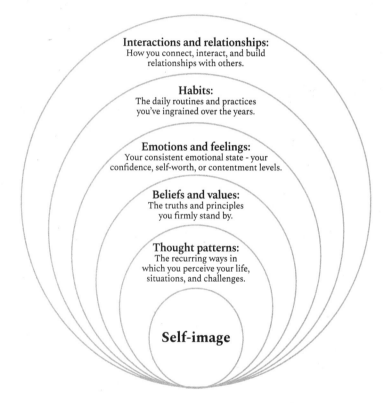

The Layers of Your Self-Image

When our self-image is fixed, it's difficult to change any of those outer layers. For example, if we attempt to alter the habits layer without addressing the self-image core, it soon becomes very challenging. It's like sticking a patch on a leak without fixing the source. So, the key is to change the self-image first, and that will naturally change and align the layers beyond it. To bring about real, lasting transformation in any of these layers, it's crucial to first address and change your self-image.

Remember, every word and thought we have holds enormous power. Everything we do is ultimately a power negotiation with ourselves, from *Will this purchase empower or disempower me?* to *Will this relationship serve my highest self or lead to self-destruction (loss of power)?*

Your self-image is at the center of everything you experience in your life. Your self-image is the reason you are who you are, that you do what you do, that you think the way you think, and that you produce the results you produce. When you change that fundamental aspect of who you are and how you think of yourself for the better, everything else becomes easy.

I'm sure you've heard people say that changing your habits is the most important step in transforming your life, to achieving more. And that discipline is the only thing you need to create the life of your dreams. However, habits and self-discipline are simply two pieces of your self-image; you can't focus only on those things if you want to truly create lifelong, lasting change.

Maintaining self-discipline and the right habits requires immense willpower, too. Of course, it's possible to transform areas of your life using these tools, but it's so much harder than simply tweaking your self-image so you truly feel that you're the kind of person who *naturally* does those things that you want to do, who naturally achieves those things that you'd like to achieve.

Change the Way You See Yourself

Altering your core self-image by perceiving yourself in a more positive light changes your habits, raises your motivation levels, and increases your desire to be disciplined. You'll see so much more success with this approach, and in a fraction of the time. It's the foolproof way to truly transform, without falling off track as much as you would if you focused solely on changing your actions through pure willpower and discipline.

If you deeply *believe* that you're the kind of person who makes millions, who has a healthy, fit body, who enjoys fulfilling relationships, who loves the work they do, who is balanced and level-headed, who is positive and motivated, then what's stopping you from activating these beliefs as truth?

If you truly *believe* that these qualities are intrinsic to who you are, it will be easy to wake up every morning and work on your goals. Why? Because your goals are part of you. It will be straightforward to make the financial decisions that this version of you would make. If you receive a bonus at work, say, you may choose to invest that extra money instead of spending it carelessly.

And if while you're eating out you see yourself as a healthy, fit person, you'll naturally lean toward the healthier dishes on the menu which align with how you see yourself and what you value. You won't feel restricted when eating these foods, because they're simply what you enjoy. You won't tell yourself that you're ordering the healthy option because you're trying to be 'good.' You'll do it because it's just what you do. It's part of who you are.

If you view yourself as the kind of person who has fulfilling, mature, and loving relationships, you'll speak differently during times of disagreement with your partner. You'll naturally hold yourself to a different standard in your friendships. You'll instinctively make the effort to call family members more often because doing so equates with the actions of someone who has deep and beautiful relationships. Even our simplest goals (such as following a morning routine, moving outside for 20 minutes a day, spending less time on our phones) become effortless. We do them without even realizing it.

Once you change your self-image to a more positive one, you notice that all the goals and dreams that you desire to achieve in your life have to do with being a new version of yourself. It's not actually about changing those things 'matter to matter.' The trick is to *be* the new self who *already has* these things in their day-to-day life – who already gravitates toward these good decisions that you'd like to make.

The way you see yourself creates the standard for what you experience in your life. Some say that your standards create your life. I say that your self-image creates your standards. Your self-image creates your habits; your self-image dictates your actions; your self-image determines your beliefs; your self-image is a predictor of your success. Show me your self-image. Explain to me who you believe you are as a person at the core, and I'll show you your future. It doesn't matter where you come from, and it doesn't matter who you believe you once were. All that matters is who you choose to be from this point onward.

CASE STUDY: LAURA

Laura, a 33-year-old subscriber to the Activations app, recently shared with me how transforming her self-image changed her life. For years, Laura's sense of self-worth was almost non-existent. Growing up in a household marked by emotional abuse, she'd learned to stay small, avoid attention, and silence her own voice. Every choice she made – from avoiding meaningful relationships to taking lower-paying jobs – was shaped by a belief that she wasn't good enough. She carried a crippling fear of being judged, rejected, or simply not measuring up.

But things began to change when Laura started exploring the idea that her self-image wasn't set in stone. Through Activations, daily journaling, and learning how we can change our identity, she began to understand that she wasn't bound by the limitations her past had imposed on her. She started envisioning who she wanted to be, rather than who she'd always believed she was: Someone capable of owning her voice, standing up for herself, and embracing her worth.

A pivotal moment came when Laura, who had spent years trapped in an emotionally abusive relationship, finally made the decision to leave. She'd stayed because she'd believed she didn't deserve better, that this was the best she could get. But as her inner work deepened, she began to see herself as worthy of love and respect. On the night she packed her things and walked out the door, she wasn't just leaving a toxic partner, she was leaving behind the version of herself who had settled for so little.

The transformation didn't stop there. Once free, Laura pursued passions that she'd long suppressed. She'd always loved painting but had never dared to share her work, convinced that others would ridicule it. With her newfound sense of self, she entered a local art exhibition. Standing in front of her own piece at the gallery, seeing people admire and connect with her work, she felt an unfamiliar but empowering sensation: pride. She realized that she no longer needed external validation to feel worthy – her self-worth was something she had built from within.

Laura's journey wasn't easy or quick, but it was life changing. She now lives in a way that honors the person she's become – confident, empowered, and unafraid to take up space. By shifting her self-image, Laura reclaimed her life, proving that no matter where we start, we have the power to create the person we want to be.

The Psychology of Self-Image

In the realm of self-transformation and personal growth, few names stand out as prominently as Dr. Maxwell Maltz's. Often seen as the father of self-image psychology, Dr. Maltz's groundbreaking insights into the human mind have left a big mark. He believed that the concept of self-image was the most significant discovery of his generation and that how we see ourselves (our self-perception) fully influences our actions, behaviors, and the trajectory of our lives.

Dr. Maltz's bestselling book *Psycho-Cybernetics* was released in 1960, way before the self-development boom began. In it, he introduced the idea that all people possess a mental self-image that determines their limits and capabilities, and ultimately what they end up becoming in their life. His findings assert that negative perceptions of our self-image can and will hinder our potential, while a positive self-image can unlock a large amount of success and happiness.[1]

Throughout his work, Dr. Maltz emphasized the power of visualization and the mind's capacity to reshape one's reality. The principles outlined in *Psycho-Cybernetics* were foundational in the modern self-help and psychology fields, a testament to the deep influence of Dr. Maltz's work. It was my grandfather who introduced me to Dr. Maltz's book. He's a man of few words who usually hides behind crude humor and small talk, but in one of the only deep conversations we've ever had, he told me that the book changed his life after he read it 50 years ago. Coming from a family of Ukrainian immigrants who started out with nothing in Canada, he rarely discussed his rise to success in real estate, but he credited much of it to the insights he gained from this book.

Change Can Be Effortless

Once you train your current self-image to align with your new Future Self self-image, achieving everything that you desire in life becomes effortless. The hard part is choosing the new self-image and committing to becoming it. Once you've achieved that, you need to practice being that version of you every single day. Later in Part II, I'll show you what it takes to change your self-image and share the high-level tools and strategies of transformation to use, including visualization and harnessing the incredible power of the mind.

Society has told us our whole lives that change and being the best version of ourselves is hard. *I'm here to tell you that it's not.* In fact, I don't allow that idea to even register as a possibility in my mind. I've lived life believing it's hard, and

I've lived life believing it's not. On any given day, I'll choose to believe that change can be effortless. Because it really is, if you believe it.

Now, I'd like to clarify a few things before we move on to the rest of Part II. When I use the word *effortless*, I don't mean that it doesn't take work to get to where you want to be. Even the lives of the most successful people (that of a multimillionaire who is happy, fit, lucky, joyful, and abundant, say) reflect the truth that a positive self-image requires effort to maintain.

The caveat is that doing the things to maintain the lifestyle you want isn't hard if you have the self-image to reflect it. Here's an example. Someone believes they are a runner and calls themself a runner. They socialize with other people who are runners. Because that person is a runner, their self-image reflects that. They don't always feel in the mood to go on a run, but they do it anyway. And the thing that pushes them to get out of bed, put on their running shoes, and go on a 10-mile run in the mornings? That's their self-image. It's not their willpower. It's their self-image influencing their decisions.

Sure, self-image can influence willpower, but it's not even worth considering willpower most of the time because if you have the self-image of someone who sticks to their plans and to their commitments to themselves, you're not going to have a problem with willpower. All positive momentum stems from having a positive self-image. If you're having trouble reaching your goals or being the type of person you want to be, don't beat yourself up, thinking that you lack willpower and discipline. Simply restructure your belief system and boost your self-image by using the tools in the coming chapters.

When you naturally do something with ease, even if it's not the most pleasant thing in the world, that's when you know that thing is aligned with your self-image. For example, if you find it very difficult to keep your house clean, it's because you have the self-image of somebody who doesn't believe they're an organized and clean person. It's not difficult for someone like Marie Kondo to keep her house clean; in fact, she finds it quite therapeutic.

I'm sure it doesn't take grueling effort and intense willpower for people who believe that they're organized humans to unload the dishwasher each morning. Or clean as they go while cooking. But for the person who believes that cleaning is hard and takes a lot of effort and time, it's going to be more difficult. This is tied to their belief system, their self-image, and their conditioned patterns. But it becomes effortless once we decide to align ourselves with the self-image of our Future Self, which you'll learn how to do in the coming chapters.

Changing My Self-Image

I'd like to share a personal example of the way self-image is linked to absolutely everything in our life, and how it dictates the results of what we're working toward. Sometimes it's hard to see this, but when we do, we can't unsee it.

Activate Your Future Self is the first book I've written. The concept for it occurred to me years ago, but for some reason I didn't truly commit to writing it until recently. Although I'd practiced self-image-based transformation techniques for years, I still couldn't see that I was holding myself back from writing this book simply because my self-image wasn't yet aligned with being an author. So, I consciously changed my self-image from someone who was too busy to write her first book to someone who is a writer, an author who writes with ease.

I began to condition my subconscious programming to believe that writing is easy for me. Writing a book doesn't need to take long, and it doesn't have to involve excruciating effort. I have a Post-it note on my computer with these affirmations:

- Writing this book is easy. The content for this book flows out of me effortlessly.

- I get so much quality content written every time I sit down to write.

- I'm an incredible author. I speak in a clear, concise, motivational way that truly impacts my readers.

- I love writing this book. Being in the flow makes me deeply happy. I really enjoy communicating through words.

These affirmations became my anchors, keeping me in a state of flow and inspiration. Whenever I felt stuck or uninspired, I'd read these words and remind myself that the challenge was not as difficult as I thought. These simple reminders helped me to break through the mental blocks that so often stop writers in their tracks. As a result, I completed the book in just three months. Before I even started, I had a strong, intuitive sense that *now* was the time to write. I knew this book was bigger than me – it was something I needed to share with the world. To align with that purpose, I had to reshape my beliefs and craft a self-image that matched the accomplished author I envisioned myself becoming.

I did so much more beyond writing affirmations on Post-It notes, though, and I'll continue to share these tools throughout this book. But for now, I hope this example highlights the reality of this work. It never stops. Changing my self-image has gotten me to where I am today, and it will continue to get me to where I want to go.

✦

If all this still feels too simple or unrealistic, and your mind is already coming up with reasons why achieving what *you* want can't be effortless, take a moment to question those thoughts. Is your mind trying to protect you? For most of your life, you've likely believed that success only comes through struggle, right? And by now, you understand that your brain resists change – it craves the familiar, even if that means staying stuck. But if you're willing to engage with the practices I'm sharing, I promise you'll see the difference. As the saying goes, 'Don't knock it till you try it.' So, give it a chance – just try it.

You're so powerful. You must believe in your power, believe in the power of your mind, believe in the power of the influence your self-image holds. You can create the life of your dreams. It doesn't need to be hard; it can become natural and effortless to you. It can be enjoyable and exciting. Believe in yourself. Believe in your potential.

CHAPTER 4

Your Beliefs, Thoughts, and Emotions

What we believe about ourselves, others, and the world around us governs our lives, influencing our thoughts, our emotions, our energy, and our actions, and therefore shaping our reality. Understanding some of the mechanisms, both spiritual and scientific, behind this process can be a powerful catalyst for personal growth.

Have you ever made progress in a certain area of your life only to find that it's short-lived? Perhaps you lost weight, made more money, or committed to a new, positive change in your life but then, without even realizing it, reverted to your old behavior within weeks or months. Author and speaker Ed Mylett has an explanation for why this happens. He likens our personal identity to an 'internal thermostat' that determines the direction of our lives and says that by working on our thoughts and beliefs about ourselves we can initiate long-lasting changes.[1]

Adjust Your Internal Settings

Mylett asks us to first think about the way a room thermostat functions: 'external temperatures may temporarily enter the room when you open a window, but the thermostat will always bring the temperature back down to where you set it.' And then explains that 'our internal thermostat works the same way. Good and bad external things will happen, but you'll always return to the default temperature on your thermostat.'[2]

We have different internal thermostats for every area of our lives – from our career achievements and the amount of money we have in the bank, to the quality of our relationships, and the state of our health – each with its own default temperature setting: the one with which we're most comfortable. The problem, Mylett says, comes when people put immense effort into achieving external results without first adjusting their identity, or their internal thermostat.[3]

We've all heard stories about people who suddenly amass wealth only to quickly lose it; it's estimated that more than 70 percent of lottery winners have spent their fortunes within a few years.[4] This is likely because they didn't raise the temperature of their internal thermostat before being exposed to this wealth, and therefore deep down, they felt unworthy of it and didn't know how to handle it.

This internal thermostat is the subconscious standard that decides what you allow and what you don't allow to happen. If your external achievements surpass the default setting of your internal thermostat, you'll instinctively regulate them to return to where you were. Let's say your internal money thermostat is set at 60 degrees, a temperature that feels comfortable in terms of your bank balance. If you venture too far above or below this, an unfamiliar feeling of discomfort descends. For example, if you get a $3,000 bonus at work and that brings your internal thermostat to 62 degrees, you'll do something to bring it back down to 60 degrees because it feels unfamiliar and uncomfortable; you might splash out on a vacation or accumulate small expenses. On the other hand, a sudden large expense, like an unexpected bill, might drop you to 58 degrees, and this would likely motivate you to save more, pick up extra shifts at work, or feel a push to start that side hustle.

And if your internal relationship thermostat is set at 40 degrees, this reflects certain standards and boundaries. If a partner doesn't align with these, you'll instinctively feel the need to address the imbalance or seek a different relationship that takes you back to your default setting.

So, it's essential to work on elevating our identity and our self-image – raising the temperature of our internal thermostats – right now, so it's aligned with our ultimate Future Self, motivating us toward better relationships, improved health, and even amplified success.

Watch Your Language

How we talk about ourselves matters much more than we may realize, and the words we use are important because they reflect and reinforce our deeply held beliefs about who we are. The 'I can't' vs. 'I don't' theory demonstrates the profound influence of our self-image and the words we choose to affirm it. To understand how this principle works in real life, meet Amy and Joe...

Amy has never seen herself as a smoker and has internalized a non-smoker identity. When offered a cigarette at a party, her response is instinctive: 'No, thanks. I don't smoke.' This statement stems from her deeply ingrained self-image. She doesn't see herself as a smoker, so the act of smoking doesn't align with her identity. Her rejection is straightforward and effortless.

Joe, on the other hand, has been trying to quit smoking for years. Despite his best efforts, he still views himself as a smoker on a deeper level. When offered a cigarette, he responds with, 'I can't. I'm trying to quit.' Joe's language reflects his internal struggle. The phrase 'I can't' suggests restriction and denial, implying that smoking is still a part of his identity. This makes his journey to quit smoking immensely challenging.

The difference between the phrases 'I can't' and 'I don't' is subtle yet significant. 'I can't' implies an external restriction or a temporary state of denial, often leading to feelings of deprivation. 'I don't,' however, is a declaration of identity and autonomy. It aligns with how you see yourself and your choices, making it a more powerful and sustainable approach.

Your words are powerful tools.
Use them to build the self-image you
desire and to support the changes
you want to make in your life.

The language we use shapes our self-image, which in turn influences our behavior. When you say, 'I don't' instead of 'I can't,' you're not just changing words, you're changing your perception and beliefs about yourself. This subtle shift can transform your approach to habits, goals, and personal growth. For instance, instead of saying, 'I can't eat junk food,' try saying, 'I don't eat junk food.' The latter aligns with a healthy self-image and makes it easier to stick to healthier food choices. It also places the power with you.

Start noticing the language you use to talk about who you are and who you are not. Replace 'I can't' with 'I don't' and observe the impact. This small change can lead to a significant shift in your self-image, your self-perception and, consequently, your behavior and propel you toward becoming your Future Self.

Accessing the Power of the Mind

There are many perspectives on the ways that our beliefs, thoughts, and emotions influence and create the lives we lead, and in this section, we'll explore several of these, allowing you to connect with the one that resonates most with you. We'll begin with the placebo effect, a mysterious phenomenon that's long held the attention of both scientists and self-improvement enthusiasts because it demonstrates the powerful relationship between the mind and body and how what we believe impacts our physical and psychological states.

The Placebo Effect

A placebo is a 'dummy' treatment that contains no active ingredients, such as a sugar pill. Researchers use placebos during clinical studies to understand the effects that a new drug might have on a condition. One group of participants receives the active drug, while the other is given a placebo, which looks exactly like the active drug but is completely inactive.

None of the trial participants know if they're taking the real treatment or the fake one. Remarkably, however, some participants respond to the placebo and report improvements in their condition, even though it shouldn't have any effect on the body. This response is called the placebo effect, and it's thought to be largely due to the person's beliefs or expectations that they're getting the real treatment rather than the fake one.[5]

When used in the realm of personal development, the placebo effect highlights the importance of having a strong, positive self-image. When you fully believe in your abilities, your potential for growth, and now, in your new Future Self identity, it's a given that you'll manifest those qualities in your life. This isn't just wishful thinking; scientific research has shown that holding empowering self-beliefs can lead to a new self-image, a new perception of the world, better performance, increased resilience and improved qualities, and therefore, a radically better and more successful life.[6]

And you don't even need to take a sugar pill to experience these results. All that's required is a powerful drive to overcome your old negative beliefs and ingrain your new positive Future Self beliefs into your subconscious (see Old Self Beliefs vs. Future Self Beliefs on page 37). By deliberately shifting your mindset and focusing on positive beliefs, you can begin to reprogram your brain.

Neuroplasticity, the brain's ability to reorganize itself throughout our lives by forming new neural connections, or pathways, allows for this transformation. By consistently practicing the techniques I share in Part II and throughout the book, you'll create new neural pathways that support your desired self-image, external experiences, and emotional state. And over time, these practices will lead you to a new, unlimited, and extraordinary life.

If You Believe It

The neuroscience that explains the placebo effect offers further insight into the relationship between our beliefs and our experiences. When we hold a strong belief or expectation, our brain releases neurotransmitters and hormones, such as dopamine and endorphins, that can lead to measurable changes in our physiology.[7] This process demonstrates that the power of belief is not just psychological – it can also have tangible effects on our physical bodies.

A fascinating example of this phenomenon is seen in a study conducted by Dr. Guang Yue, an exercise psychologist at the Cleveland Clinic Foundation in the US.[8] Participants were divided into two groups, one of which engaged in physical exercise while the other simply visualized themselves performing the same exercises. After several weeks, the group that exercised physically experienced a 30 percent increase in muscle strength, while the visualization group saw a 13.5 percent increase in muscle strength, despite not engaging in *any* physical activity!

This research demonstrates the powerful effects of visualization and belief, providing further evidence that the mind can significantly influence the body. We'll talk more about visualization later in this chapter.

In another groundbreaking experiment conducted by Harvard psychologist Ellen Langer in 1981, a group of men in their 70s were invited to spend five days in a secluded retreat that had been styled to replicate exactly the environment of 1959, complete with period-appropriate furniture, decorations, music, media, and entertainment.[9] The men were instructed to fully immerse themselves in the experience, acting as if they had traveled back in time and actually *were* the person they'd been 22 years earlier. At the end of the study, the participants exhibited major improvements in various physical and mental health measures. They had more energy, increased grip strength, better posture, and improved cognitive abilities; some even reported significant improvements in their vision and hearing. All in just five days.

Using the Mind to Heal the Body

Shifting our mindset to a more positive one even has the potential to cure physical pain. One of my biggest inspirations and one of the greatest expanders in this space is Dr. Joe Dispenza. I've had the privilege of attending many of the retreats he's led, and I feel compelled to share part of his incredible journey here because it demonstrates the immense power of the mind.[10]

In 1986, Dispenza was hit by a truck while cycling in a triathlon and suffered multiple spinal fractures. Doctors told him that he'd likely never walk again and recommended surgery to fuse his spine with rods. However, because of his strong conviction that 'the power that made the body, heals the body,' Dispenza chose a different path. Instead of opting for the operation, he left hospital and embarked on a rigorous mental and emotional journey to heal himself through the power of visualization and focused intention. This decision would change his life, and subsequently, those of millions of others.

Over the course of 10 weeks, Dispenza spent two hours twice a day visualizing the reconstruction of his spine, holding on to the firm belief that his body could heal itself if he could successfully communicate this intention to his subconscious mind. With all odds against him, Dispenza's unwavering determination began to make a difference in the physical. Incredibly, he regained sensation and mobility in his legs, and within 12 weeks, he was able to stand and walk again. By the end of his healing journey, he'd made a complete recovery, defying all medical expectations. Today, Dispenza dedicates his life to helping people do the extraordinary, just like he did.

✦

Now, as you reflect on this inspiring personal story and the scientific evidence that proves the power of the mind to change our beliefs, consider the vast array of options that await *you* in life. The possibilities are endless, and your future potential is unlimited. Could you heal yourself from within? Could you achieve wealth and abundance through the power of belief? Is it possible to fall deeply in love with every aspect of your life? You must embrace the power of your mind to unlock the countless opportunities that lie ahead on your journey to living your ultimate life.

Reprogram Your RAS

Now let's explore a physiological mechanism that can help us pay more attention to things that align with our positive self-image and goals: the Reticular Activating System, or RAS. The RAS is a complex network of nerve pathways situated at the brain stem that decides what we consciously see and focus on; it filters out everything that the brain doesn't deem 'interesting' or 'essential,' drawing our attention to what it's been previously taught.[11]

Imagine trying to process all the sensory information in your daily life all at once, from the sound of the dishwasher to the cars honking outside and the breeze from the open window. That's where the RAS comes in, ensuring your brain stays focused on what's important. And what it deems important is programmed by what you regularly think about, what you focus on, your beliefs, and your goals. This means that if you think positive, goal-oriented thoughts, your RAS will highlight opportunities and information that support those goals. On the flip side, if you constantly worry or dwell on negative thoughts, your RAS will bring more of that into your conscious awareness.

The key to reshaping your reality lies in training your RAS to focus on what you desire.

Imagine you're thinking about buying a red car and suddenly, you start to see red cars everywhere. It's not that there are more red cars on the road; rather, it's that your RAS is now tuned to red cars, and it's showing you what you're looking for. When you flood your brain with new ideas, practices, and thoughts, it rewires your RAS to start noticing things that previously went unnoticed.[12] This primes your mind to align with your Future Self, helping you spot opportunities that guide you toward the person you're becoming and the success you seek in daily life.

But this system also works on a larger, more complex scale. Imagine if your RAS was programmed to support the belief 'I'm not attractive.' You'd constantly notice subtle cues that seem to confirm this idea – a glance from someone that you interpret as judgment, or moments where others receive compliments while you go unnoticed. At the same time, your brain would filter out evidence to the contrary – times when someone does show interest, or when you look great but fail to acknowledge it. In a self-fulfilling prophecy, holding the belief that you're not attractive means your brain will quite literally show you proof everywhere that this is the truth.

When it's reprogrammed consciously, your RAS is a mechanism that can and will present opportunities to you and you'll start seeing them everywhere. Reprogramming your RAS is going to be the first step in priming you to recognize and seize those opportunities.

The RAS in Action

Remember the 'Lucky Girl syndrome' TikTok trend that started a few years ago? People who followed it began to see themselves as lucky, and as a result, they noticed more positive events and opportunities in their lives. The more they believed in their luck, the more their RAS highlighted situations that confirmed this belief, creating a powerful cycle of new opportunities and positive things happening. This shows how the RAS can be consciously directed to bring about changes in one's life – good or bad!

Here's another example of how the RAS can help us succeed. Imagine you want to be promoted to a management position at work. If you start dressing professionally and working as hard as you would in that more senior position, your boss will begin to see you differently. Subconsciously, your boss will think, 'They take their job seriously. They're a hard worker.' When the time comes to choose a new manager, you'll likely be at the top of their mind.

When you focus on your goal and act *as if* you've already achieved it, your RAS starts to filter in opportunities and behaviors that align with that goal. As you get noticed for your hard work and professionalism, and eventually earn that promotion, it reinforces your belief in your capabilities. This, in turn, strengthens the programming of your RAS, creating a positive feedback loop. Your belief in your potential grows, your RAS continues to highlight opportunities for success, and you keep progressing. We'll talk more about acting 'as if' and how it can help consolidate your Future Self, next.

Essentially, the RAS creates a domino effect in every area of your life. Focused thoughts and beliefs shape your perception and actions, leading to real-world achievements that reinforce those positive beliefs, and the cycle continues. The RAS offers a neuroscientific explanation of the concept of manifestation.

The Magic of Acting 'As If'

What you need is already inside of you. You already hold those qualities and potentials. Remember, the idea is to be your Future Self right now. The only thing you need to do is to *act as if* you already are the person you want to be, whatever that is: positive, happy, healthy, loving, fit, hard-working, confident, and successful. With constant, daily practice you will eventually transform into your Future Self.

Acting 'as if' is a powerful cognitive therapy technique in which individuals adopt the mindset and behaviors of the version of themselves that they aspire to be, even when faced with self-doubt and obstacles. It's a zero-cost, immediate strategy to tap into the energy and potential of our Future Self. I use this tool a lot in my life – during big business meetings; in my relationships; and to boost my self-confidence. This technique is one that was instrumental in transforming my life into what it is today.

Acting as if you are your Future Self essentially allows you to be like them in that moment. The more you act like them, the faster you'll become them. Just as with any skill, the more you practice, the closer you get to mastering it. Acting as if you already have what you want isn't about playing pretend or ignoring your current reality. It's about realizing that your point of power lies in focusing on the present moment and deliberately directing your attention toward what you want, knowing that your reality will eventually follow suit. By embodying the traits and behaviors of the person you aspire to be, your Future Self, you gradually become that person.

How to Act 'As If'

Acting 'as if' means thinking, speaking, and feeling like the person you want to be. Picture yourself as the lead character in a movie. Every scene, every interaction is a chance to channel your Future Self. How would they hold themselves? Speak? Eat? Sit? Walk? Dress? You must believe in the character – you must truly believe that this person exists within you, and it's just a matter of bringing them out.

Throughout your day, pay attention to the way you handle yourself and how you react to various situations. Turn it into a fun game whenever you find yourself bored, like when you're in line at the grocery store or driving to work. Turn the mundane everyday moments into opportunities to experience what it's like to be your best self.

Acting 'as if' is also a fantastic tool for boosting your confidence when you're experiencing doubt or facing challenges. Whenever a problem arises and you feel yourself reacting negatively, ask yourself, *How would someone who already has what I want react to this?* This ongoing self-reflection will help you to align your actions with the beliefs, thoughts, and feelings of your desired Future Self.

The trick to acting 'as if' is to really *feel* it in your body and experience all the sensations this would cause. It means genuinely behaving, feeling, thinking, and being that person. The easiest way to begin is with simple actions because these lead to new thoughts and beliefs. And although this technique is fun to use, it isn't just a game – it's a habit that truly elevates your energetic state. When you're thinking new thoughts, embodying a new vibration, and truly being the essence of your Future Self in everyday moments, transformation is magnetized toward you.

This process helps you tap into the deeper potential within you. Every time you act 'as if,' you're reinforcing the belief that you're capable of change. This belief is crucial because it shapes your reality. Your brain starts to create new neural pathways, making these new behaviors and thoughts more natural over time.

Acting 'as if' also helps us to break free from limiting beliefs – false beliefs about ourselves that place limitations on our actions and prevent us from pursuing our goals and desires. Often, we hold ourselves back because we believe that we aren't capable of achieving our dreams. But when you act as if you have already achieved them, you challenge these beliefs and prove to yourself that you can be different. You can also adopt new habits, change your mindset, and create a new reality.

Acting 'as if' is an incredibly easy, low-barrier way to prove this to yourself. It also helps to create a positive feedback loop. When you act as if you are your Future Self and see positive results, it reinforces your belief in your ability to change. This, in turn, motivates you to continue acting as if, leading to even more positive outcomes.

This technique is about more than just changing your behavior. It's about changing your self-image. It's about *becoming* the person you want to be, not just *doing* the things they would do. This requires a shift in mindset and self-perception. You need to start seeing yourself as capable, worthy, and deserving of your desires.

> *As you continue to act as if you are your Future Self, you'll find that your external reality starts to change to match your internal state.*

Opportunities will arise, people will respond to you differently, and you'll find yourself moving closer to your goals. This is the power of aligning your actions, thoughts, and emotions with your desired future.

One of the most significant benefits of acting 'as if' is that it allows you to experience your desired future in the present moment, which is deeply motivating and empowering. You don't have to wait for external circumstances to change to feel happy, confident, or successful. You can generate these feelings now by embodying your Future Self. Remarkably, this is precisely what will get you there.

Visualize It, Be It

Let's delve into two more powerful cognitive practices you can use to change your beliefs about yourself and what you can achieve: visualization and mental rehearsal. These are essential tools for personal development, enhancing our self-image, income, relationships, performance, and more, helping us reach our goals.

In Chapter 1, when you visualized your Future Self through the lens of the five pillars of life – mental, financial, physical, spiritual, social – you experienced firsthand the power of using mental imagery. Visualization goes way beyond daydreaming – it's a disciplined practice that effectively links your deepest desires with actionable steps.

And mental rehearsal is a way to prepare your mind and body to enact the Future Self scenarios, actions, habits, attributes, and behaviors you visualized and wrote about when you created your Future Self, by going through them in your mind beforehand, optimizing your Future Self readiness. These techniques work synergistically to empower you to achieve your goals, by changing how your brain works and what you attract energetically.

The benefits of visualization have been extensively studied by science and the technique is endorsed by a wide range of experts, including neuroscientists, quantum physicists, and psychologists. And for our purposes, it positively affects specific areas that support our Future Self energy.

Neuroscientists have found that when we perform an action in our mind, it engages the same neural pathways that are used when we perform the action in the physical, effectively tricking the brain into thinking we're having a real-life experience.[13] For example, fMRI (functional magnetic resonance imaging) research shows that when a person visualizes themselves playing the piano, the same areas of the brain associated with piano playing are activated.[14]

From the perspective of psychology, visualization can have a profound impact on motivation, confidence, and achieving goals. By visualizing a desired outcome, we can increase our motivation, leading to improved performance. For example, psychological studies have shown that athletes who visualize performing successfully before competitions tend to perform better.[15]

Visualization engages the subconscious mind, working in our favor even when we aren't paying attention, actively solving problems and tapping into our creative mind.[16] Ever been on a walk to clear your mind, only to have a rush of creativity and motivation follow? That's the power of the subconscious mind at work when we clear it of negative thoughts and make room for the potentials that await us.

From a quantum physics perspective, the act of observation can affect the outcome of events. And as visualization can be seen as a form of focused observation, this suggests that by visualizing a specific outcome, we can influence the probability of that outcome occurring.[17]

Visualization and Acting 'As If'

Research has shown that living an experience in your mind, visualizing it, is almost as powerful as doing the work in real life.[18] Studies have also shown that when you train your personality to 'act' in a certain way, over time you'll likely start taking all the steps that this new personality would take, without even thinking about it.[19]

As you practice being your Future Self, combining visualization and acting 'as if' will turbocharge your efforts, and you'll feel more confident and comfortable when you come to do the things that will bring you success. For example, if you behave like someone who is highly disciplined, you'll become highly disciplined. You just need to believe in it. Visualization also triggers the Reticular Activating System (RAS). When you both visualize and act as if you're already the person you want to be, you create a powerful shift in your brain. This triggers your RAS to focus on opportunities and behaviors that align with your desired self.

As we've discussed, neuroscience shows that the human brain doesn't differentiate between vivid mental imagery and actual physical experience. This means that if you're constantly feeling unworthy, worrying about your health, and perpetuating fear in your life, you're actually making your body go through the physical experience of it – whether or not it's true. The crazier part is that this can actually *cause* disease progression within the body.[20]

Our bodies believe what our minds tell us, so it's incredibly important that we choose our words and thoughts wisely. You must choose what you think about every single day, make sure it's positive, make sure it's healthy, and make sure it's something that you actually want. Without evidence that something's wrong, you shouldn't be thinking the worst.

Like acting 'as if,' visualization can also help you to overcome limiting beliefs. If you repeatedly fight your limiting beliefs by flooding your brain with new thoughts and feelings, you'll eventually replace them with new, positive beliefs that will help you succeed. For example, if your current limiting belief is that you aren't a confident person, you'll invariably fail at making business connections. Visualize being a confident, engaging person who's great at talking themselves into business deals. If you do this regularly, you'll slowly notice magic begin to unfold in your life.

Mental Rehearsal

Mental rehearsal is a practice session that takes place in the mind, preparing us for action in the real world. It's a technique in which we imagine ourselves performing a specific task or reaching a particular goal, or for our purposes, being our Future Self right now.

One famous story about the benefits of mental rehearsal was told by US actor Jim Carrey. At the start of his career, Carrey wrote himself a $10 million check for 'acting services rendered,' dated it five years in the future and kept it in his wallet. Over the following years, Carrey would drive up to Mulholland Drive in LA, an exclusive neighborhood home to Hollywood stars, every night and visualize himself receiving the success he desired, with directors being interested in him and people praising his work. Remarkably, five years later, he found out he was going to make $10 million for a movie role. This mental rehearsal not only made him feel better but also helped him align his actions with his goals.

I, too, have successfully used mental rehearsal to create change in my life. Around 10 years ago, I was struggling with binge eating and began using mental rehearsal to cure myself of it. Here's the process I followed. First, I closed my eyes and brought myself into a pre-binge state that had been triggered by feeling stressed, overwhelmed, and sad. I visualized and felt exactly what it was like to be in this state and getting the craving to binge. I then pictured myself taking a different path – drinking a big glass of water, calling a friend, going out for a walk, or journaling. I really felt and saw my pride and satisfaction in taking this new path. Finally, I repeated the steps until it felt less uncomfortable – it usually took three repetitions.

Many of us, especially women, struggle with disordered eating habits. I spent years trying to heal my binge eating through traditional therapy and even hypnotherapy, but nothing truly worked until I discovered mental rehearsal. I realized that binge eating was a coping mechanism my brain had relied on, and it was up to me to break the cycle.

By using mental rehearsal to create a new thought loop, like the one I've just described, the brain will start offering a different choice in a real-time moment of craving. After doing this exercise a few times, I found that when I next craved a binge, a new thought appeared: there was another option. Although I initially caved in and binged, the thought was there. The next time, after more practice, I chose the new path and dealt with my emotions in a healthier way. The more I did this exercise, the more the urge to binge faded. Before long, I stopped binge eating altogether.

Mental rehearsal was a key tool during my journey to becoming my Future Self, too. Whenever I felt scared, nervous, or anxious about attending a significant meeting or about speaking in general, I'd close my eyes and imagine myself in the setting – whether it was an interview room, a restaurant, or a stage. I'd see myself speaking confidently, maintaining good posture, and engaging with the other person/people. I'd experience calmness, clarity, and confidence as I visualized myself performing well, seeing the positive reactions from my audience, date, or interviewers.

By repeatedly picturing yourself achieving your goals, you train your mind to respond with confidence and clarity in real-life situations.

By repeatedly visualizing a successful outcome to the situation in which I had to speak publicly, I trained my mind to respond with confidence rather than fear. When the real event arrived, I found myself effortlessly speaking clearly and confidently, just as I'd rehearsed it in my mind. Mental rehearsal allowed me to step into these situations as my best self, turning nervous energy into a powerful performance.

These are just a few ways that mental rehearsal can help you to become your Future Self, but the possibilities are limitless. The practice helps you take new actions, making lasting change possible. It not only boosts our self-esteem; thanks to the brain's neuroplasticity, it also strengthens the neural pathways associated with the new habits and behaviors we're focusing on. By visualizing positive outcomes and practicing new behaviors in your mind, you make it easier to act in line with your goals in real life.

Whatever aspect of your Future Self you're striving to embody – be it breaking a bad habit, mastering a new skill, or stepping into a more confident version of yourself – mental rehearsal and visualization will be key to your success. The more you practice, the more ingrained these new neural pathways become, leading to lasting transformation and a more empowered you.

Let Go of a Victim Mentality

It's not uncommon for people to see themselves as victims when they experience setbacks, or when life doesn't go their way. Characterized by negative self-talk, blaming others for our problems, and a lack of personal responsibility, this victim mentality can be truly toxic, hindering our personal growth and preventing us from reaching our full potential.

When we see ourselves as victims, we perceive the world through a lens of helplessness and hopelessness. It feels as if our lives are dictated by external events, and that we're powerless to make any changes. For example, if we're not far enough along in our career, we assume it's because of factors beyond our control – our upbringing, lack of connections, or bad luck. This mentality convinces us that success is unattainable, and we remain stuck in a cycle of self-pity and inaction. However, by shifting our mindset to one of empowerment and taking responsibility for our actions, we can break free from this cycle and unlock our true potential.

Adopting a victim mindset can harm our mental health, our relationships, our ability to create success and our overall well-being. It might be difficult to accept, but the reality is that we're not victims. We hold the power to create the lives we desire. We're far from helpless, and we can make intentional choices to improve our circumstances. However, to achieve this, we must first overcome a victim mentality.

As I've been explaining in this chapter, your beliefs have a far greater impact on your brain than you might think. I know it might be challenging to wrap your mind around this concept but clinging on to a victim mentality will become a self-fulfilling prophecy. If you believe you're a victim, your subconscious will search for reasons to validate this belief – and what we know about the RAS is evidence to support this. In order to release a victim mentality, we must retrain our RAS. Becoming aware of our negative self-talk, our tendency to blame others, and our avoidance of personal responsibility is crucial.

Let me gently guide you through this. I encourage you to consider the idea that releasing a victim mentality will open up a world of possibilities for you. By acknowledging and taking responsibility for your reality, you'll be one step closer to creating the life you've always desired.

Take Responsibility for Your Life

A person with a victim mentality often attributes their lack of happiness and success to external factors or other people, perpetually living in the shadow of their past experiences. It's a cycle. They might say things like, 'It's not my fault,' 'Life is unfair,' or 'I'm always unlucky.' Victims will consistently blame external circumstances and refuse to take responsibility for their actions.

As I mentioned in the introduction, taking 100 percent responsibility for your life means acknowledging that you have control over your reactions, decisions, and, ultimately, your life's direction. Even when situations aren't ideal, you can control how you respond to them. By adopting this mindset, you empower yourself to turn adversities into learning experiences and setbacks into setups for your future success.

**When you focus on the way you respond to
life's events, you take control of your destiny.**

There's an equation in Jack Canfield's book *The Success Principles* that can help you counteract a victim mentality: Event + Response = Outcome (E + R = O).[21] Put simply, if you're not satisfied with the results you're currently getting, you need to change your response (R) to the events (E) around you until you achieve the desired outcome (O).

This mindset shift requires a high level of honesty with yourself and the willingness to let go of draining habits like blaming external circumstances or complaining. Instead of feeling like a victim, helpless and letting circumstances dictate your life, you end up empowering yourself to create the outcomes you desire.

CASE STUDY: ELIZABETH AND JAKE

Let's look at two real-life stories that show how letting go of a victim mentality can help us in our evolution to our best selves.

Elizabeth grew up in a turbulent household, and for years, she believed her difficult childhood was the reason she struggled in her relationships and career paths. Doing personal development work made her realize that she had the power to rewrite her story. Instead of seeing herself as a victim of her upbringing, she took responsibility for her future, got therapy, and worked on herself at a deep level. Today, she's a successful entrepreneur who advocates for mental health.

A car accident left Jake severely physically impaired, but instead of letting this unfortunate circumstance dictate his fate, he took charge of his healing. At first, he felt overwhelmed by the idea of being confined to a wheelchair, which would mean he could no longer play golf. Jake had dreamed of becoming a professional golf player, and he was on his way to achieve that goal throughout high school and college, competing in semi-pro tournaments and making a name for himself.

After accepting his new reality after the accident, Jake was unwilling to leave the golf world behind. So, he channeled all his expertise into coaching up-and-coming pros. Though he coached from his chair, he discovered he had an exceptional ability to train because of his passion and drive.

His unwavering dedication to living the best life he could not only sped up his recovery but it also inspired everyone around him.

He eventually left the wheelchair behind and regained most of his physical abilities because of the positive mindset he chose to adopt. The victim mentality never sunk its claws into his spirit, so he was able to remain empowered, physically and mentally. Today, Jake still coaches but also spends a significant part of his career as a motivational speaker, sharing his journey of taking responsibility and overcoming adversity.

Imagine two paths. The first, which represents a victim mentality, is filled with blame, resentment, and stagnation. The second path shines brightly and is lined with empowerment, growth, and success. Which path would you choose for a fulfilling life?

Envisioning living without the shackles of a victim mentality is *extremely* liberating. It's a world where challenges are seen as opportunities, where every setback is a stepping stone to greater success, and where *you* are in the driver's seat. How empowering is that?

Lose the 'I'll Be Happy When...' Mindset

I'll be happy when I start earning $10,000 each month.

I'll be happy when I lose 15lb and can fit into my old jeans.

I'll be happy when I finally move into a bigger home.

I'll be happy when that person I like finally notices me.

I'll be happy when I have some more time alone and I'm not working as much.

I'll be happy when I finally like myself.

The disturbing truth behind the 'I'll be happy when...' mindset is that it's an endless loop without an exit. And you can easily become addicted to it. You'll start to achieve these 'goals,' but when you do, you'll just keep wanting more and more, never feeling truly satisfied. You'll never experience the truth of success and happiness because all you've done is teach yourself how to feel dissatisfied with your life.

The trick is to experience *right now* all the emotions that you want to feel deep gratitude for in your future life. This will prime you for the exciting moment that occurs when you actually reach your goals. You'll have felt worthy before, and you'll still feel worthy then. Your happiness won't be contingent on any external validation; it will come from within. And this is all linked to self-love: love yourself enough to allow yourself to experience good things, even before you've achieved what you desire.

Your Future Self is looking back on the life you're living right now and wishing they could relive it. Not because they wish that they could change things. The opposite, in fact: they want to experience living in this phase of your life again. Let yourself be happy. One of the biggest regrets that older people admit to having is that they didn't live more in the moment and allow themselves to be happy more often. Let yourself fall in love with your life, *now*.

Think Like an Investor

Another mindset shift that will help propel you on your journey to cultivating a positive self-image is to regard yourself as an investor in every aspect of your life. The Investor's Mentality is a powerful concept that can revolutionize how you perceive and approach your life. An investor allocates time, money, energy, and resources *now*, without expecting immediate satisfaction, in anticipation of greater rewards in the future. They trust that, with time and consistency, their investments will yield significant results. This mindset can be applied not only in our finances but also in our personal growth, self-improvement, health, and beyond.

CASE STUDY: ELLA, TAYLOR, AND LOGAN

I'd like to share the stories of a few people who have embraced the Investor's Mentality in different areas of their lives as they activate their Future Self.

Ella is very fit and healthy, and she invests in her body by consistently working out, even when she doesn't feel like it. She eats nutritious foods, passes on the donuts at work, and wakes up early to do a Pilates session at home before the day starts. Ella understands that her commitment to a healthy lifestyle will have long-lasting benefits for her physical and mental well-being. She knows that the time and effort she puts in now will pay off in the form of a stronger, healthier, and more vibrant version of herself.

Taylor is committed to reaching a certain net worth by the time she turns 35. To achieve this goal, she's saving and investing her money, taking on side hustles, committing to changing unhelpful thoughts and beliefs around money, and working diligently on her business. She makes sacrifices in her social life, opting for lower-cost activities like having her best friend over for a home-cooked dinner and a movie. She recognizes that the money and time she saves now will grow exponentially, helping her to reach her financial goals. Taylor's Investor's Mentality keeps her focused on the long-term benefits of her choices, knowing that each step she takes today brings her closer to the Future Self she envisions.

Logan has a history of poor mental health but has chosen to adopt the Investor's Mentality to improve his well-being. For him, this means doing breath work every morning, journaling, spending time with friends, and enjoying being in nature. He recognizes that engaging in these activities consistently will help him avoid falling back into a dark place. By investing in his mental health, Logan ensures that he can maintain a balanced, positive outlook on life, and continue to grow as a person.

By adopting an Investor's Mentality in one or multiple areas of their lives, these individuals see the real results of their dedication.

It's essential to think about the long-term consequences of our actions. The choices we make in the present moment will have a massive impact on our future; that's just life. By asking yourself which is worse – momentary self-discipline or long-term regret – you're forcing yourself to think critically about the choices you're making.

In the moment, it may seem easier to give in to temptation or avoid putting in the effort required to truly step into your desired Future Self. We're naturally programmed to 'go the easy route' in life. But in the long run, those choices always end with disappointment and regret.

Adopting an Investor's Mentality means that when you stray from your plans to live a better life, you'll find it easier to return to them. By prioritizing long-term success over short-term satisfaction, you embody the Investor's Mentality, and this pushes you to take the necessary steps toward personal growth and ultimate life fulfillment. With this state of mind, absolutely anything is possible.

The fact that you picked up this book and have made it this far proves that you're already investing in yourself! Rather than looking for shortcuts, you're willing to put in the time and effort now, to reap the results later. Choosing yourself and the future that you want through moments of heightened self-discipline can be challenging, but it will lead to great rewards. By staying focused on your goals and pushing through discomfort while you're becoming your Future Self, you're setting yourself up for success in the long term.

Energetic Vibrations

Have you ever found that when you're around someone who's bubbling with anger or frustration that you struggle not to become influenced by their negative emotions? That's because they're projecting a powerful signal. The same goes for someone emanating sensuality, or one grappling with challenges, or even one emanating serenity and love. You perceive these emotions because they're tangible, palpable things.

An increasing amount of scientific research demonstrates that our emotions carry various frequencies and vibrations that significantly influence our well-being and the world around us.[22] The positive ones, like love, joy, gratitude, are higher frequency vibrations. But the negative ones, like fear and anger, are lower frequency vibrations.

So, if we're replaying the same thoughts and emotions day after day, we're essentially broadcasting the same vibration on a loop. Our past keeps shaping our future because we're ensnared in an energetic rut. But here's the upside: We possess the ability to change our vibration and shift our frequency. It's all about transforming how we think and how we feel.

Many of us grew up in environments where we were prevented from fully experiencing and expressing our emotions, which created a disconnect within ourselves from our own feelings. Some of us were taught that negative feelings were something terrifying that we should avoid at all costs, or which we'd be punished for having. This interference with our natural feeling state has made us unable to identify our true feelings.

Or perhaps we feel shameful about the emotions that arise. If you were raised in an emotionally invalidating home, you probably never had the chance to understand what different emotions felt like in your body as you experienced them, and you didn't learn how to trust your gut feelings in order to set boundaries.

Releasing Negative Feelings

In his books *Power vs. Force* and *Letting Go, the Pathway of Surrender* the late psychiatrist and spiritual teacher Dr. David R. Hawkins explored the profound impact of emotional vibrations on our lives, including their effects on our overall well-being, health, and success. He developed a Map of Consciousness, a groundbreaking energy scale that assigns distinct values – from 0 to 1,000 – to different emotions.[23]

According to Dr. Hawkins, emotions such as shame, guilt, and fear vibrate at frequencies below 200. These emotions drain our energy, compromise our health, and create obstacles to achieving our goals. For instance, shame, which is at the bottom of the scale with a frequency of 20, can lead to self-destructive behaviors and a sense of unworthiness. On the other hand, emotions that vibrate at frequencies above 200, such as courage, neutrality, and willingness, mark the beginning of constructive and positive states. As we move up the scale, we encounter higher vibrational emotions like acceptance, reason, love, joy, peace, and enlightenment, which significantly enhance our vitality, creativity, and overall quality of life.[24]

Dr. Hawkins emphasized the importance of letting go of lower vibrational states to raise our level of consciousness. He explained that by surrendering negative emotions and allowing ourselves to experience higher frequencies, we can transform our lives. This process involves recognizing and accepting our emotions without resistance, allowing them to pass through us, and ultimately dissolving their negative impact.[25]

Dr. Hawkins' research highlights the correlation between our emotional state and our physical health. Higher vibrational states are associated with improved immune function, reduced stress, and enhanced overall well-being. Conversely, lower vibrational states have been proven to lead to chronic stress, illness, and a host of negative health outcomes. And in terms of success, people who operate at higher vibrational frequencies tend to be more resilient, creative, and effective in their personal and professional lives. They attract positive experiences and opportunities, and their higher frequency states inspire and uplift those around them.[26]

All of this is closely aligned with the concept of the biofield, which we explored in Chapter 2. Our biofield interacts with the biofields of others and the environment, creating a dynamic exchange that influences what we attract into our lives. So, when we cultivate higher vibrational emotional states such as love, joy, unlimitedness, and peace, and practice acting as our Future Self daily, our biofield emits positive energy, which acts as a powerful magnet for similarly positive experiences and opportunities. This is why people with elevated emotional states often seem to encounter more favorable circumstances and are more capable of manifesting their desires. This is also another explanation for the Law of Attraction.

Our feelings are our personal truth: little messengers arising from within, helping us navigate life! The goal is not to dismiss any emotion or keep it from happening; it's to learn how to keep moving forward despite what happens. Once you begin to know what you are feeling and why, you can then advance this process to create your Future Self.

To create the emotional state you want, it's essential to make a conscious decision to feel and embody it right now. By doing so, you align with the emotions of your Future Self, rather than remaining stuck in the patterns of your past. When you pair a strong, clear vision of your future with the positive emotions that reflect it – such as abundance, health, and vitality – you begin to train your brain and body to adapt to this new reality, just as many people unconsciously train themselves to stay attached to the past. This shift allows you to pave the way to a new future.

Condition Your Mind

Classical conditioning is a type of unconscious or automatic learning that occurs when a person or animal experiences an automatic response whenever they encounter a specific stimulus. In essence, it is learning by association. The method was first studied in the 1890s by the Russian physiologist Ivan Pavlov. While experimenting with dogs, he noticed that they began to salivate before seeing their food, triggered by the mere sounds associated with feeding time, such as the approach of a food cart. By ringing a bell as a signal before feeding, Pavlov found that the dogs could be conditioned to associate the sound of the bell with food, leading them to salivate at the sound of the bell alone, even without food present.

Classical conditioning is a powerful tool for personal transformation. Consciously integrating this technique into your daily routine will supercharge your efforts to become your Future Self. The Activations on the Activations app are specifically designed to create a conditioned response through association. For example, listening to an Activation while making breakfast and getting ready for your day, or while out on a walk, will remind you to act as your Future Self.

If you do this repeatedly, soon enough you won't even need the Activation to feel unlimited, alive, and abundant. Over time, this daily practice will effortlessly condition your mindset and behavior toward becoming the person you aspire to be. It's about teaching yourself in the everyday, seemingly mundane moments, and essentially tricking your brain to bypass your Old Self's resistance to new behaviors or thoughts.

Classical conditioning can also be used to help you recover from setbacks. Try rewarding yourself for any small amount of progress you make when you revert to being your Future Self after falling off track. This could be something like treating yourself to a massage after reaching a milestone in a new project. Or even something small like allowing yourself to enjoy a favorite treat or take a relaxing break. Gradually, your brain will start associating setbacks with opportunities for growth and a feel-good moment.

Accessing the Law of Attraction

As you're probably aware, the Law of Attraction is a universal spiritual principle that states 'like attracts like.' The basic idea behind it is that our thoughts, emotions, beliefs, and actions act as magnets, attracting experiences, opportunities, and individuals that resonate with the same vibrational frequency. This vibrational frequency affects our energy and the energy around us, shaping how we perceive situations and influencing how others respond to us.

The Law of Attraction states that when you focus intently on something, you can attract experiences and people that align with that focus. Your current life is a direct consequence of your thoughts, so if you pay close attention, you'll see the connection between your thoughts and the reality you've manifested.

The Law of Attraction responds to the thoughts you project into the world. Therefore, if you keep thinking that you have no money in your bank account, you'll continue to attract a lack of money. If you feel depressed due to relationship problems, you'll draw more depression into your life. This universal law operates continuously, whether you're aware of it or not. Therefore, it's crucial to keep your thoughts focused on what you want, rather than what you don't want.

Shift your focus to positive thoughts and emotions, and you'll begin to attract positive experiences and people. This isn't just wishful thinking – it's a powerful tool that, when used correctly, can transform your reality. Remember, you're the creator of your own life, and by aligning your thoughts with your desires, you can shape your future in extraordinary ways.

Change Your Assumptions

In a similar way to the Law of Attraction, the Law of Assumption is the principle that what you assume is true will become your reality. Introduced by the US philosopher, author, and teacher Neville Goddard in the 1950s, it suggests that our thoughts and beliefs shape our experiences, and that by assuming we already have what we desire, we can manifest it into our lives.

Harnessing the energetic power of assumption can profoundly influence our actions and the way others respond to us, creating a self-fulfilling prophecy. For instance, if you assume that someone dislikes you, you might avoid them and act defensively around them, even if they initially had no negative feelings toward you. Your behavior can eventually cause them to feel hostile toward you, fulfilling your original assumption.

Here are three more examples of how the Law of Assumption can shape your reality:

- **Assuming you won't get the job:** If you enter an interview room believing you won't be hired, your lack of confidence and enthusiasm will negatively impact your performance. You might stumble in your responses, fail to showcase your strengths, and miss opportunities to connect with the interviewer. This negative assumption will likely lead to a poor interview outcome, making it less likely you'll receive an offer.

- **Assuming someone doesn't find you attractive:** Believing that someone isn't attracted to you can cause you to act awkwardly or withdraw when interacting with them. Your lack of confidence and engaging behavior can decrease their interest in you, even if they might have been attracted to you initially. By assuming rejection, you inadvertently create conditions that make rejection more likely.

- **Assuming you'll fail an exam:** If you go into an exam convinced that you'll fail, you'll likely experience heightened stress and anxiety, which can interfere with your ability to focus and recall information. This mindset might lead to inadequate preparation or second-guessing your answers, ultimately resulting in a lower score. Your assumption of failure becomes a reality through your actions and mental state.

The Law of Assumption operates on a deeper, spiritual level by recognizing the energetic influence of our beliefs. When you assume that a particular outcome will take place, you align your energy with that assumption, attracting similar energy from the universe. This alignment creates a powerful vibrational frequency that shapes your experiences and interactions. For instance, when you assume abundance and success, your energy resonates with these positive states, attracting opportunities and circumstances that reflect this belief (the Law of Attraction). Conversely, assuming scarcity or failure emits a lower vibrational frequency, drawing in negative experiences and obstacles.[27]

> *By consciously aligning your assumptions*
> *with your best interests, you will create a*
> *reality where that actually happens.*

This spiritual understanding shows the interconnectedness of our thoughts, energy, and experiences, encouraging us to take responsibility for our assumptions and their impact on our lives. By changing your assumptions to align with your desired outcomes, you can create positive shifts in your reality. Instead of assuming failure or rejection, assume success, confidence, and positivity. This shift in mindset can influence your behavior and interactions, attracting the outcomes you desire. The Law of Assumption empowers you to take control of your thoughts and beliefs, guiding you toward a reality that reflects your true aspirations.

In order for assumption to work in the process of becoming your Future Self, you must see your wishes as already being fulfilled. You must be able to imagine what you want vividly and feel as though you already have it. As I stressed earlier, it's the *feeling* that matters most. It also helps to focus on feeling because it crowds out all unproductive thoughts.

Remember, life is always happening *for you*, not *to you*. Stop feeling like a victim and assume instead that the universe is on your side. Then you'll begin to see that the challenging, difficult, and sometimes devastating situations you experience may simply be leading you to your ultimate destiny and fulfillment in life.

✦

Spiritualists call it manifestation.

Scientists call it quantum physics.

Religious people call it prayer.

Psychologists call it self-image psychology.

Atheists call it the placebo effect.

This diverse array of evidence converges on a singular truth: *Our inner world creates our outer world.* By understanding and harnessing this power, we can consciously create the life we desire. It's not just about believing in one explanation or concept over another; it's about recognizing the universal principles that underpin them all. This holistic understanding allows us to take control of our destiny, knowing that we have the capacity to shape our reality with our thoughts and energy. Lean into whichever of these tools intuitively feels right to you.

You Get to Choose Your Reality

What if you become your Future Self right now, and never look back? What if you embrace the energy of your ultimate desired Future Self and transform everything in your life? Shift your perspective and truly test out how it would feel if this were your reality: You are your Future Self right now. Really, right now, as you're reading this, *feel* like your Future Self!

Once you get familiar with this feeling, it becomes easier, and the results get stronger. If you keep it up for a while, soon enough, you'll find yourself becoming more your Future Self than your Old Self. You'll have created the results you've always wanted by hacking the system – and by system, I mean your brain, your subconscious mind.

To embody your Future Self energy and position yourself on the road to true, lasting transformation, you need to do this: **Be you – that you – now.** Teach yourself to become your Future Self now, *in this moment*. Before you're ready, before you have it all figured out, before you want to. Push through the resistance of your Old Self. Ignore the excuses and the 'logical' reasons why this theory is silly or why change is hard. Don't listen to the Old Self! It doesn't want to change. The true you, your ultimate Future Self, is the person who picked up this book. This version of you can feel the potential you truly hold.

You get to choose your reality. You get to choose how hard or how easy it can be. Your destiny is in your own hands, so would you like to believe that it can be effortless? If you knew deep down in your bones that everything you desire isn't that far away, you could, for a moment, embody that energy of possibility, put aside all your beliefs, opinions, thoughts, and emotions for just a moment and open your mind to the possibility that your reality could be different.

I promise you that once this core belief changes, becoming your Future Self can be effortless. Life will become so much brighter. You'll feel it as you go through your day – you'll feel this deep trust, this deep knowing that everything you create is up to you and there is truly nothing holding you back. When you begin believing that what you want can actually happen, and that it's just part of who you are, a part of why you're here on Earth, you'll experience an energetic shift on a physical level.

Your relationship with your life will change. Your relationship with the world around you will change, too – you'll see magic and opportunity everywhere. Your perception of the world will change, in a better, more beautiful and expansive way. When your energy is aligned with effortless transformation and success, more of that comes into your life naturally. This could be your RAS at work, or it could be a combination of the RAS and quantum physics, or attracting what you desire because your energy is magnetically aligned with it. I personally believe it's a mix of quantum physics, energetics, and neuroscience. Whatever you believe, there's a reason to back it.

Imagine that you're standing at a crossroads. To one side, there's a familiar, paved path – smooth, predictable, well-traveled. On the other, there's the Bunny Trail – a path that's less clear, winding through the underbrush, inviting yet unknown. Choose to step onto the Bunny Trail. It will feel difficult at first but remember that starting is the hardest part.

Once you keep choosing the Bunny Trail, it becomes easier and easier to travel along it. The underbrush gets flattened out, and you become more comfortable with taking this route. Now envision a fresh, new way of thinking, one that's different from your current mindset. Choosing that way of thinking feels like taking the Bunny Trail. The more you take it, the less uncomfortable it becomes, and the possibilities for growth stretch out infinitely.

Change is tough at the beginning, but it gets simpler each time you choose the Bunny Trail over the familiar paved path. And the more you choose it, the more it becomes an easier path to follow. The more it becomes an established path.

CHAPTER 5

Your Environment

Your environment is more than just your physical space; it encompasses the company you keep, the content you consume, and the tools you use. This chapter explores the profound impact that our surroundings have on our reality. From cluttered spaces to the distractions of technology, and even the dynamics of our social circles, each element subconsciously imprints on the mind, influencing how we think, behave, and perceive the world.

This becomes even more significant when you're cultivating your Future Self. The environments you choose either reinforce old patterns or actively support the mindset, habits, and behaviors necessary for you to become the person you envision. By curating an environment that's aligned with your Future Self, you accelerate the process of transformation, allowing your surroundings to mirror and support your desired future.

By understanding and intentionally curating each element of your environment you can significantly alter your thoughts, feelings, behaviors, and self-image – often without even realizing it. I'll show you why it's essential to be aware of your surroundings and teach you how to make conscious choices to cultivate an environment that positively impacts your life.

Consider Your Social Circle

Let's start with the big one: the people in your life. The motivational speaker Jim Rohn famously said, 'You are the average of the five people you spend the most time with.' The social circles and groups that you associate with truly determine your current and your future reality.

It's naïve to think that we can have close relationships with negative people who don't have the same goals and dreams as we do and believe that we have enough self-control and power not to be affected by these negative influences. None of us is that strong, and given that humans are wired to imitate our surroundings, why would we put so much effort and work into trying to fight that? If the people with whom you spend most of your time are not where you want to be, or on their journey to getting there alongside you, they are directly inhibiting your success.

Let's say the people closest to you behave as if they are victims. They think small and are content to live an average life. All they do is watch TV after work and drink alcohol on the weekends to forget how unhappy they are. If these are the types of people you're surrounded by, it's going to be incredibly difficult for you to be the most vibrant, happy, abundant, and hard-working version of yourself. Conversely, if you surround yourself with people who think big, who have huge goals and aspirations, who are supportive and loving, who are ambitious, focused, and lead healthy lives, then without even trying, you'll start replicating this yourself the longer you spend time with them.

Surround yourself with people who uplift you, challenge you, and inspire you to become the best version of yourself.

Changing your social circle isn't easy, but it's necessary for your growth. Start by engaging in activities and communities that align with your interests and goals. Go to workshops and retreats, join clubs, or participate in online groups where you can meet like-minded people. It's crucial to seek out those who are on a similar path or have already achieved what you aspire to.

The Influence of Other People

In psychology, the theory of mimetic desire suggests that people desire things because someone else did first. Therefore, many of our goals and desires are influenced by what those in our social circle desire or value. In addition, the theory of emotional contagion suggests that emotions can be 'spread' from one person to another. So, if those around you are positive, non-victim-mentality people, you're more likely to feel optimistic, while being around negative individuals will drag you down and you'll begin thinking negatively without even realizing it.[1]

Your romantic partner plays an even more significant role in shaping your self-image and life. They influence your daily habits, emotional state, and overall outlook more than anyone else.[2] This is why it's essential that you choose a partner who supports your growth, shares your vision, and uplifts you. Their effect on the trajectory of your life is profound, so it's crucial to ensure that they're aligned with your goals, aspirations, and the way you want to live.

The Imitation Game

We tend to imitate the posture, mannerisms, and behaviors of the people we spend time with, without being aware of it.[3] When we like someone or hold them in high esteem because of their social status, personality traits, or other reasons, we tend to imitate them more than others. For instance, if you're having lunch with a friend who speaks slowly and methodically, you might find your speech slowing down too, even if you're typically a fast talker. Or if you go on a walk with a friend, you might notice that your stride and arm swing become like theirs. At times, we'll even copy the behavior of people we don't particularly like.

What makes us susceptible to this unconscious imitative behavior? Research has found that those who are more concerned with others, depend more on others, feel closer to others, or want to be liked by others tend to adopt other people's behavioral traits to a greater extent.[4] This can be attributed to insecurity and a lack of a defined true self. When we feel less confident about who we are, we 'wear' the traits of another person that we feel are more socially acceptable than our own. We're also trying to strike a balance between a desire for distinctiveness – feeling unique and different from others – and a desire for assimilation, belonging or feeling similar to others. When we feel too unique or too similar, we're motivated to regain the balance, which is why we fluctuate in this mimicry.

The point I want to emphasize is that you should become more aware of the people you spend time with and how each person significantly influences you, both subtly and overtly. If you notice that their behaviors aren't in line with the vision you have of your Future Self, it's time to shift to a new circle of influence. This will help you cut through the chaos and negative mental chatter, allowing you to focus on your growth and transformation.

The Advice You Should Never Take

One of the best pieces of advice I received during my transformation into my Future Self is to never take advice from someone who doesn't have what you want. For example, why would you heed relationship advice from someone who's never been in a thriving long-term relationship? It makes no sense to listen to them if they lack the experience and success in the area in which you seek to improve.

Similarly, why would you accept business advice from someone who's never owned a business? They can't provide the insights and strategies needed for real achievement. And health advice from someone who eats donuts for breakfast and doesn't do any exercise? It's like hiring an obese personal trainer. Our natural instincts tell us not to take advice from someone who doesn't embody the results we seek.

Of course, it's different if your very close family members and friends offer constructive advice, because their insights come from a place of love and concern. However, for the most part, I advise you to follow this rule as you continue on your journey to living your most abundant, happy life.

I remember the big family dinner when I announced my plan to drop out of university, move to London, England, and become an entrepreneur by creating an online magazine. I could see the doubt in everyone's eyes. Although I was 18 years old, to my family, I was still a young girl with unrealistic aspirations. My uncle even said, in front of everyone, something like, 'I give it six months. You'll be back in no time after realizing how silly that little dream really is.'

The funny thing about my success journey is that no one really believed in me, except me. My parents were supportive, but I knew they thought that the odds were slim. Essentially, everyone else in my life thought I was delusional. Thankfully, I'd built up my self-esteem and strengthened my self-image before embarking on this path. And I ended up blowing them all away. My uncle had never moved away from his hometown or created a successful online venture, so why would I listen to him? I knew I needed to stay focused on my goals and trust in my vision.

Spending time with friends, mentors, and other people who possess the qualities and level of success that you aspire to will allow you to draw on their knowledge and experience to propel yourself forward. Their stories, insights, and practical advice will help build the blueprint you need to create your own success.

The 'frequency match' concept created by Penney Peirce in her book *Frequency: The Power of Personal Vibration* is valuable for understanding this.[5] It suggests that you should align yourself with people who match the energy and frequency of the future you desire. This alignment will help you stay focused and motivated on your path to success – magnetizing it toward you.

Keep Your Distance

If you find it challenging to distance yourself from the people who have a negative influence on you, start by gradually reducing the time you spend with them. You don't need to sever ties completely. Instead, limit your contact with them and seek out more positive influences to balance out your social interactions.

Even if you can't find a new social circle in person immediately you can start surrounding yourself digitally with inspiring and motivating content. We're so lucky in today's world that we have unlimited access to millions of positive resources – from books to videos and podcasts – that have been created by people who align with your future (even if they don't know you exist!) So, in the interim, as you start moving away from the old group who no longer align with your Future Self, you can inundate your mind with this new information, with these new people, and these new views of the world as you try to find deep and meaningful in-person connections.

But how do you sever ties with lifelong friends or family members who you care for deeply but who don't align with your Future Self or are simply not good influences? This is an incredibly tough question to answer. It doesn't need to be all or nothing; I've learned that slowly fading away from those who don't make me feel good or don't support my big dreams and aspirations has been my best bet. Of course, I still see some of these people at family functions or rare reunions, but the point is to minimize the time I spend with them.

Declutter Your Space

Our physical surroundings have a profound impact on our life, shaping our mental clarity, well-being, and overall success. The spaces we inhabit are deeply connected to both our mind and our emotions, a fact supported by both science and psychology.

Neuroscientific studies suggest that our brains thrive in organized environments. Clutter overloads our senses, reduces our ability to focus, and drains our cognitive resources.[6] When you're surrounded by clutter, distractions, and chaos, it's challenging for your mind to remain focused and calm. From a psychological perspective, a tidy environment can act as a mirror to our inner self, reflecting a sense of control and order.[7]

Imagine your surroundings as a mirror of your mind – when your space is clean and organized, it promotes peace, focus, and efficiency. A clean space is a sanctuary, a place where thoughts flow freely and creativity blossoms. Keeping your space tidy isn't just about aesthetics; it's about creating a setting where you can be your best self. When your space is messy, it's not just the room that's disordered: often, your thoughts and emotions are, too.

Think about the energy held by physical things in your environment. Old clothes, an overflowing email inbox, unread texts, and old furniture can carry stagnant energy that bogs you down. Removing old clutter (both technological and physical) not only refreshes your space but also brings in new energy for the things you actually want.

> *The act of decluttering creates a powerful signal to your subconscious that you're making room for new opportunities and growth.*

Just think about how refreshing it feels to clean out your closet or organize your workspace. That sense of accomplishment and renewal isn't just in your mind; it's a real, tangible shift in your energy. When you take the time to sort through your belongings and let go of what no longer serves you, you're also letting go of mental clutter. This process is incredibly liberating and can lead to increased mental clarity and emotional well-being. Think of it as a form of self-care; by taking care of your environment, you're taking care of yourself.

Creating an environment that supports your goals goes beyond just decluttering. It's about intentionally designing your space to reflect the life you want to live. This could mean setting up a dedicated workspace that's designed for your productivity, arranging your living area to encourage relaxation and connection, or even creating a vision board that visually represents your dreams and aspirations (more on this soon). Each of these elements contributes to a holistic environment that nurtures your growth.

Create Environmental Cues

Including cues within your space that remind you of your Future Self is a powerful strategy to keep your goals and aspirations at the forefront of your mind. Start by understanding what truly inspires and motivates you. After getting clear about what you want in life in Part I of the book, you should now have a strong sense of your goals and your Future Self persona. Use this clarity to guide you in creating environmental cues that keep that version of you in focus.

Inspirational quotes are a great place to begin. Choose words that resonate deeply with you, which speak to your future and the person you want to become. Print them out and place them where you'll see them often - on your bathroom mirror, above your desk, or on your fridge. I write out quotes or words that motivate me on Post-it notes and keep them on my water bottle or on the back of my phone. Every time you read these quotes, they'll serve as a gentle nudge, a reminder of what you're striving for and why it's worth the effort.

Images can also be incredibly powerful. They help you to visualize your Future Self and the life you want to manifest. Find or create images that represent this vision: they could depict the dream home you'd love to own, a place you want to travel to, or an image that symbolizes the career success you want to achieve. You could bring all these images together on a vision board and place it in a prominent spot where you'll see it daily; this will help reinforce your commitment to your aspirations, keep your motivation high, your focus sharp, and your goals top of mind.

As well as quotes and pictures, you could also incorporate into your environment other elements that resonate with your Future Self. This could be specific colors that energize you, scents that calm and focus your mind, or music that inspires creativity and drive in you. Each of these can contribute to physical surroundings that constantly reinforce your goals and the version of you that you're in the process of becoming.

Your workspace is another critical area where you can integrate environmental cues. Set it up in a way that reflects your future achievements. For example, if you intend to become a successful entrepreneur, arrange your desk to mirror that of someone who's already achieved what you aspire to. This could include keeping it clean and organized, displaying awards or certificates, and surrounding yourself with books and materials that inspire you. Your workspace should not only be functional but also a place that makes you feel empowered and capable of achieving your goals. Plus, if you have an inspiring workspace, you'll want to spend more time there!

The science behind this approach is compelling. Studies have shown that our brains respond strongly to visual stimuli. When we see something that aligns with our goals, it activates the brain's reward system, releasing dopamine, which enhances motivation and focus.[8] By surrounding yourself with visual reminders of your aspirations, you're essentially priming your brain to stay committed and focused on your objectives.

These environmental cues do more than just remind you of your goals – they also shape your self-image. By consistently exposing yourself to these cues, you begin to internalize the beliefs and attitudes of the person you want to become. This process creates a positive feedback loop in which seeing your goals reinforces your belief in your ability to achieve them, which in turn motivates you to take the actions necessary to bring them to fruition.[9]

The key to making environmental cues effective is consistency. Ensure that they are highly visible and present in your daily life. The more you see them, the more they'll influence your thoughts, emotions, and behaviors. Over time, these small, consistent reminders can lead to significant changes in your mindset and progress toward your goals.

It's important to understand that your physical environment is not static; it's dynamic and should evolve as you do. Regularly reassess your space to ensure it continues to meet your needs and supports your goals. This might mean decluttering every three to six months, updating your inspirational cues, or rearranging your furniture to better suit your current lifestyle. By continually refining your environment, you maintain a space that remains fresh and is conducive to your ongoing growth and success.

Dress Like Your Future Self

Wearing clothes that your Future Self would choose is more than just aesthetics; it's a powerful catalyst for change. Studies have shown that the clothes we wear significantly influence our mood, confidence, and even how our brains work. This phenomenon, known as 'enclothed cognition,' suggests that there's a direct link between what we wear and our mental state.

A study published in *The Journal of Experimental Social Psychology* found that participants who wore white lab coats performed better on attention-related tasks than those who didn't.[10] The mere act of wearing a piece of clothing associated with attentiveness and care influenced their cognitive performance. Taking this into account, just imagine how much impact dressing in a way that aligns with your Future Self could have on a daily basis!

> *When you dress like the person you aspire to be – your Future Self – you're more likely to act, think, and feel like that person.*

It will boost your confidence, enhance your mood, and sharpen your focus, making you more productive and successful in your day-to-day life. Remote workers in particular could benefit greatly from the practice of dressing like their Future Self. Dressing intentionally while working from home can build your desired self-image and keep you in a mental space that will raise productivity. Research shows that we perform better when we feel and look better. For example, a study done by the University of Hertfordshire in the UK found that people who dressed smartly felt more confident and performed better in their tasks compared to those who dressed casually.[11]

Clothing also acts as a reflection of our inner energy. When you choose outfits that resonate with your ultimate Future Self, you exude energy that aligns with your goals and desires. Dressing intentionally can become your new favorite morning ritual, setting the tone and inviting in your Future Self energy for the day ahead.

Consider a Closet Detox

Before starting to dress like your Future Self, you must ensure that your closet contains items of clothing that align with this version of you. A closet detox is a great way to achieve this. As you review each item, ask yourself, 'Does my Future Self wear this?' If the answer's no, it's time to donate, sell, or recycle it. Keep only those pieces that resonate with your Future Self – clothes that make you feel powerful, confident, and aligned with your goals. This process sets a clear intention for how you want to present yourself to the world.

While you're clearing out your closet (or any other room in the house) you can also ask Marie Kondo's question, 'Does this spark joy?' Again, if it does, keep it, if not, dispose of it. By focusing on these questions, you'll create a wardrobe and a home environment that truly reflect and support your Future Self.

Next, consider creating a capsule wardrobe. This is a collection of essential, timeless pieces that you can mix and match effortlessly. Think of it as the foundation of your Future Self's style. A well-curated capsule wardrobe ensures that you always have something appropriate and empowering to wear, without the overwhelm of too much choice. Include pieces that reflect your personal style and professional goals, from sleek blazers and tailored trousers to elegant dresses and comfortable yet stylish shoes.

As you build and refine this new wardrobe, remember that quality is more important than quantity. Invest in pieces that are well-made and versatile, items that will stand the test of time and trends. I'd much rather have a smaller closet full of stunning, timeless pieces than a large closet full of mediocre pieces that I didn't intentionally buy.

If you can't afford your dream Future Self closet right now, just know that you're still able to do this exercise. There are many stores selling high-quality pieces for a good price that can help you create the foundation for your capsule wardrobe. Then you can find a few standout pieces, whether that's through thrifting or on sale. It's about how you hold yourself, and how this clothing makes you feel. Remember that.

If you *are* financially able to invest in a major wardrobe update, hiring a personal stylist can be a great option. A stylist can help you to identify the best clothing choices for your body type and personal color palette. However, if you're not quite ready to take that step, there are plenty of online resources available that can guide you in refining your style and learning how to dress in a way that flatters you. With a bit of research, you can achieve a style upgrade on your own!

By dressing like your Future Self, you're not just wearing clothes, you're embodying your aspirations and setting yourself up for success. Your attire becomes a daily affirmation of who you're becoming, reinforcing your journey toward becoming your best self. Embrace this practice and watch how it transforms not only your appearance but also what you produce in your daily life.

Be Intentional About What You Consume

Just as what we eat impacts our physical health, what we consume mentally affects our mental health – massively. What you read, listen to, and watch subconsciously programs your mind. If you constantly feed it with negative and/or mindless content, it will change your thinking and perspective for the worse.

The brain is like a sponge, especially during the periods when we're not fully alert, like right before we go to sleep or when we first wake up. During this drowsy but still awake time the brain is in the 'theta' state, where its critical and analytical filters are less active, making it more receptive to new information. This heightened receptivity allows for the embedding of beliefs and memories, making the theta state crucial for learning, creativity, and emotional processing.[12] During this time, the content we consume, particularly negative content, has a deeper impact, embedding beliefs and perceptions that will influence our actions and decisions.

So, it's essential to be aware of what you're exposing your mind to during these times in your day. In the morning, instead of reaching for your phone to scroll through social media or check the news, try journaling, listening to an Activation, or simply reflecting on your goals. What you choose to do during this time will set you up for success in your day ahead. In Chapter 10, we'll explore a morning routine that you may want to consider adopting.

The movies we watch, the music we listen to, and the articles and books we read can evoke strong emotions or stress in our bodies. Repeated exposure to these emotional triggers can condition our mood and emotional responses over time.[13] If you're constantly exposed to negativity, your brain starts to accept it as the norm, impacting your overall outlook on life. It's sad to think that most of the world lives this way, due to the news- and drama-obsessed culture we live in.

Say No to Negative Content

There's so much information out there, so you must consciously choose what you consume. If you don't, it'll be chosen for you. When it comes to the news, it's natural that you'll want to stay in the know on events both global and local. But a few things can help you stay in a safe frequency zone while you check in.

First, while you're at home, never leave news stations broadcasting in the background. While these programs 'passively' project into your environment via visual and verbal messaging, they generate distinct energies of catastrophe, chaos, disaster, fear, inequality, division, tension, and uncertainty. I don't know about you, but I consider those energies to be *unwanted guests*. But guess what? You have the power to remove them and keep them out! It's your home, after all.

Find news sources that you feel have the least amount of bias (I know that can be difficult!) and set limits on how frequently you check in (once a week, twice a month, etc.) This puts you in the driver's seat when it comes to what information you're exposed to and when. Using a reputable news app, you can choose which news stories you want to engage with and stay away from those that will disrupt your well-being.

Set boundaries – if you need to dive into some hard-hitting political issues, set a time limit (five minutes, two stories, etc.) The goal isn't to become sheltered from what's going on. It's to prepare yourself for an encounter with unsettling content that might bring your energy down or take away your positive mood. And to remain undefeated by the forces that can send you into a spiral of negativity. In this way, you can become a better change agent in this world with your focus and determination, which will undoubtedly influence others.

Before consuming any content – whether it's on social media, a TV show, or the news – ask yourself: *Does this make me feel good and raise my energy?* If the answer's no, it's time to evaluate whether you should consume it. Be aware that the news cycle thrives on negativity because bad news draws attention, while good news barely makes the headlines. To maintain a strong mindset and a higher vibration, follow pages that specifically post uplifting news. My theory is that if something's important enough for me to know, I'll hear it from my family and friends.

I'll be honest in saying that I don't fully subscribe to the belief that we need to stay informed about world events. Tony Robbins says, 'I don't watch the news because I know that they're designed to startle you and get your attention. It's a machine that's there to make money, and if you understand that, you can step away from it and take control of your own mind.'

Many successful people avoid watching TV or consuming excessive news content because they prefer to spend their time in more productive and rewarding ways. Imagine how your life could change if you adopted a similar approach. Instead of starting your day by watching the morning news, you could play a motivational podcast or read a book that inspires you. By choosing to engage with content that makes you feel like your Future Self, you protect your energy, setting the stage for a more positive, successful, and fulfilling life.

Take Control of Your Mental Diet

Think carefully about how the content you consume influences your emotions. Watching a thrilling or scary movie may leave you feeling anxious, while a heartwarming story or funny movie, or a nature documentary, will lift your spirits and make you feel good. The articles you choose to read will provoke thought and inspire action, or, conversely, instill fear and doubt. This emotional conditioning shapes not only how we feel in the moment but also how we react to various situations in the future. Everything we consume programs us one way or another. So, instead of passively letting algorithms decide what you see or hear next, take an active role.

This book is all about being the creator of your life, and to be this, you must be the curator of what you're exposed to. Mute or unfollow accounts on social media that bring you down, lower your vibration, or are mismatched with your goals. Curate music playlists that motivate and inspire you. Read books that expand your mind and align with your ideal life. Choose movies that reinforce the values and emotions you want to cultivate.

Just as you wouldn't eat junk food all day and expect to feel great, you shouldn't fill your mind with mental junk and expect to thrive. Make a conscious effort to consume content that nourishes you. Opt for positivity, inspiration, and education.

The impact of our mental diet extends beyond our immediate mood, energy, and thoughts. Over time, the content we consume shapes our long-term habits and values, and our self-image as a whole. For example, if you frequently listen to podcasts about entrepreneurship and personal development, you may soon find yourself adopting the mindset and habits of successful entrepreneurs – without even realizing it.

> *By being intentional about what you read,*
> *listen to, and watch, you can program your*
> *mind to align with your Future Self.*

Subconsciously, you'll start setting more ambitious goals, taking calculated risks, and even speaking and portraying yourself in a way that's more aligned with this version of you. On the other hand, if you spend your days consuming content that's negative or superficial, you'll likely find yourself feeling more anxious, unmotivated, and disconnected from your true goals. You're programming your subconscious mind every single day, whether you like it or not. The content you consume plays a crucial role in your Future Self transformation. Think about what your Future Self would consume – and consume that!

Actively choosing positive, educational, and inspirational content helps you stay motivated, focused, and aligned with who you're meant to be. Remember, you hold full power to curate your mental diet, and in doing so, you shape the person you become. So, take charge, begin to make conscious choices, and see how different you feel as a result!

Reconsider Your Usage of Technology

In the past few decades, digital technology such as smartphones, tablets, and gaming systems have taken a prominent position in our lives; however, there's a darker side to our devices in general, and social media in particular, that becomes apparent only when we step away from digital technology and recognize how it has weakened us.

One of the most significant issues with social media is that using it activates the brain's reward center by releasing dopamine, a 'feel-good' chemical whose job is to increase the repetition of pleasurable behaviors such as food, sex, and social interaction. And if we spend a lot of time engaging with social media platforms, this repetitive surge of dopamine can lead to a decrease in our motivation, concentration, and overall well-being. It can even trigger an addiction-like response in the brain, with each swipe, like, and post further perpetuating the cycle of dependence and disconnection from real-life experiences.[14]

Research has shown that excessive screen time can lead to mental health issues, including severe anxiety and depression.[15] Dr. Gene Beresin, a psychiatrist at Massachusetts General Hospital in the US, suggested to one depressed teenage patient that they delete their social media accounts for a few weeks. If they still felt depressed after this period, he told them, he'd then consider prescribing antidepressants. Guess what happened? The teen felt radically different after the digital cleanse and their depressive symptoms had gone.

Many people immediately check their phone on waking, and throughout the day use it to scroll through social media or news feeds. After spending eight hours glued to a computer screen for work or education, they come home, eat dinner in front of the TV, and then scroll on their device again before bed. This daily routine, with its excessive screen time, is detrimental to our well-being because it holds us back from living a vibrant, successful, and happy life. The digital sedative numbs our senses and dampens our innate drive, leaving us feeling lethargic and brain-dead.

We're the first generations to be part of an ongoing study on the long-term effects of prolonged technology use, and so far, the results are alarming. For adults in the US, the average amount of time spent interacting with electronic screens such as smartphones, tablets, computers, TVs, and other digital devices is about seven hours per day, or 2,555 hours per year.[16] Over a typical lifespan of 70 years, this adds up to an astonishing 178,850 hours – almost one-third of our time – spent staring at screens.

If we consider that we spend about one-third of our lives sleeping, and another one-third using technology, that leaves only one-third for everything else – work, family, hobbies, and personal growth. Imagine the possibilities if we could cut our screen time in half, reclaiming that third of our life for more meaningful and fulfilling activities. This stark reality highlights the urgent need to rethink our relationship with technology to live a more balanced and enriched life.

Excessive screen time not only affects our mental health but also our physical well-being. Eye strain, poor posture, and sleep disturbances are just the beginning.[17] Have you heard the phrase 'sitting is the new smoking'? It was popularized by Dr. James Levine, a professor of medicine at the Mayo Clinic in the US, to highlight the severe health risks of our sedentary lifestyle;[18] prolonged screen time fuels prolonged sitting, leading to obesity, cardiovascular diseases, and even early mortality.

Break Away from Digital Dependency

This cycle of inactivity and digital dependency stifles our productivity and creativity, making it harder to engage in activities that foster personal growth. Even though it's now seen as 'normal,' when we let technology infiltrate our lives to this extent, we become disconnected from the people we care about and also from our authentic selves. This results in a loss of personal power and a lower energetic frequency. We're no longer attracting the ideal Future Self that's out there waiting for us to create them. Instead, we're trapped in a cycle of technological dependence that numbs us out, diminishing our inner light and our zest for life.

So, let's make our escape from this cycle and reclaim our health and motivation! Imagine starting your day without immediately reaching for your phone. Instead, you take a few moments to center yourself, set intentions, and engage in activities that nourish your mind and body. Throughout the day, you consciously limit your screen time, focusing on deep work and meaningful interactions. In the evening, you unwind with a book or a hobby that brings you joy, allowing your mind to rest and recharge. Breaking free from the grip of technology requires effort and discipline, but the rewards are immense.

By reducing our screen time and reconnecting with our authentic selves, we will raise our energetic vibration, boosting our motivation, confidence, and overall sense of well-being.

We can create a life that isn't dictated by the demands of technology but enriched by real experiences and genuine connections. We can feel more alive, more disciplined, more focused, and more joyful. Remember, life was fulfilling before the advent of smartphones, social media, and digital everything. By taking control of our technology use, we can rediscover the richness of life. Do you want to spend your one shot at life feeling numb or truly alive? The choice is yours.

Mindless scrolling on my phone is the one thing in my life to which I feel a truly addictive pull. Over the past few years, I've regularly done social media detoxes, deleting the apps for a week at a time, maybe once every one to two months. Yet once I redownloaded them, I'd struggle with the same issue. It became a way for me to disassociate, distract myself, and numb out. Recently, I decided to delete the apps for an entire year. I allowed myself the exception of logging into Instagram (my main platform, where I have a couple hundred thousand followers) every three months to post an update, then delete the app again.

I committed to this 12-month detox because of an insight I had during a journaling session. Over the next year, I'll be planning and having my wedding, completing and publishing this book, and going on some incredible trips; and after the wedding, my partner and I will begin trying to conceive. I truly want to be as ALIVE and present as possible over the next 12 months – it's going to be a magical time in my life, and I want to savor every moment!

I now have an amazing executive assistant and team that can manage my online accounts and even post on my behalf. One month in, I can honestly say I've never felt clearer in my life. I feel so much more present, and so much more ME. The first five days were hard; I'd get cravings and open my phone only to find no social media apps to scroll through, but those cravings went away.

Digital Detox Tips

If you feel inspired to go all-in and delete your social media apps, go for it. But if you want to start slow, here are some other options.

- Try a social media detox every weekend, from Friday 5:00 p.m. to Monday 9:00 a.m. Or have one for the first week of every month.

- Conduct an audit of your digital life and strip it down to the essentials on your phone and computer. While work often requires the use of these devices, it's crucial to stay on track and avoid excessive social media use and binge-watching TV shows.

- Set time limits on your apps and turn off your phone once in a while. Over time, you'll begin to lose the instinctive response to fill every moment with technology. This will take time, but you can do it. Once you do, you'll notice you're living a brighter life.

- If you feel the urge to fill the void with scrolling, this is a perfect moment to use mental rehearsal to retrain yourself and stop the cycle. Imagine your Future Self talking to you – this Future Self sees clearly into the next two, five, and 10 years and can identify this addictive stumbling block. Follow the guidance of that vibrant being who sees better for you and wants to pull you back from this abyss.

Once you've completed a detox, carefully reintroduce some things into your life without developing bad habits again. When you pick up your phone, ask yourself if you're learning, growing, and being inspired, or merely killing time. Cancel a few streaming channels. Put your phone in the kitchen at night and leave a book by your bed instead. Limit texts to friends and tell them you want to chat on the phone instead.

Breaking free from the addictive pull of social media and excessive screen time is challenging but immensely rewarding.

By taking these steps, you can reclaim your time and start feeling more and more like your Future Self. Stay committed and watch as you transform your relationship with technology and, ultimately, yourself.

CHAPTER 6

Your Decisions

So far, we've dived deep into shaping both your inner and outer worlds for a streamlined Future Self transformation. Next, we'll tackle the art of making wiser decisions in real-time. To understand how deeply your decisions impact your life, I'll begin by describing another success strategy that helped me as I became my Future Self: the compound effect.

The subject of a book of the same name by US financial expert and success leader Darren Hardy, the compound effect is the principle that our decisions shape our destiny, and that small, smart changes practiced consistently can multiply, or compound, into life-changing results.[1]

You don't need any special skills or talents to take advantage of the principle of compounding – you just need to take small, positive daily actions that are aligned with your goals and the new self-image you'd like to adopt. Maintain these small daily actions over time and you'll start to see significant progress toward your desired outcomes and goals. For example, if your goal is to improve your health and fitness, you might start by committing to taking a 20-minute walk every day. It might not seem like much, but if you consistently take that walk every day for a year, you'll have walked for more than 120 hours – a huge amount of time spent moving your body and improving your health.

The Profound Impact of Compounding

In essence, the compound effect teaches us that every decision we make matters. The principle can be applied to almost every area of our lives. Here are a few examples of how compounding works in saving and investing; health and relationships; and personal development and learning.

Make an initial investment of $5,000 in the S&P 500 stock index and add $250 every month for the next 30 years. As you may know, in the world of investment, compound interest (the interest earned on interest) can offer surprisingly large returns. With an average annual return of 10 percent, your initial investment would grow to more than $600,000! This may sound too good to be true, but it's simply the power of compounding at work; the total interest makes up 84 percent of the $600,000. The longer you wait, the more powerful the compound effect gets. Switch the 30 years to 50 years, and you'll have $8,471,927.29, with only 4 percent of these funds coming from your contributions. Meaning 96 percent of this money would be from interest alone.

If you're interested in exploring the power of compounding in making your money grow, search for 'investment calculator' online and you'll find a ton of free websites that will do the math for you. This is a fun game that I often use myself to conceptualize the potential of my future. It motivates me to continue and keeps my Investor Mentality front and center of mind.

Decide to cook homemade dinners most nights instead of ordering takeout. While it may not seem significant at first, committing to this one small lifestyle change can lead to a plethora of benefits that compound over time. Cooking your evening meals yourself means you can control the ingredients, portion sizes, and cooking methods, which will lead to a reduction in your consumption of processed foods and unhealthy additives. Eventually, this can compound into substantial weight loss, improved digestion, and increased energy levels.

Adopting this change doesn't mean that you must completely give up takeout; rather, it's a shift in how often you indulge in foods that don't contribute to your overall health. Cooking at home can also be a beautiful way to unwind and spend time with loved ones, making it a habit that not only benefits your health but also your relationships.

Commit to reading for 20 minutes a day. Over a year, that small daily commitment adds up to more than 120 hours of reading. Depending on your reading speed, you could potentially complete around 12 to 24 books in a year; over a decade, that's 120 to 240 books!

The knowledge you accumulate through consistent reading could have a profound impact on your personal growth, career, and overall life satisfaction. What if one of those books changes what you want in your career, or your relationship? What if turning off the TV at night and reading before bed changes who you become in this life? The right book at the right time can shift your perspective, change your trajectory, and suggest new possibilities that you've never even considered before.

Over the years, I've read books that have wildly shifted the trajectory of my life. As I explained earlier, *The Success Principles* by Jack Canfield empowered me to start consciously creating my life and to stop passively living it. While *Money: Master the Game* by Tony Robbins taught me the critical importance of investing my money; it ignited my passion for the stock market and shifted my focus away from 'keeping up with the Joneses.' The strategies I learned have significantly increased my savings and transformed my approach to wealth building.

I've been reading books on health and longevity since I was in my late teens, and they've taught me so much about how to live a healthier and more vibrant life. Whether it's learning about women's hormones and how to work with my cycle in *Women Code* by Alisa Vitti, discovering the secrets to living into my 100s in *Lifespan* by David Sinclair, or understanding which diets are ideal for optimal brain health and reducing the likelihood of disease in *Young Forever* by Dr. Mark Hyman, books have opened up a world of knowledge and possibility for me.

Cultivating Positive Habits

Imagine how different your life would look right now if in the past you'd decided to adopt a small, positive habit and then practiced it consistently over time – swapping your morning bagel for a smoothie; reading five pages of an educational book every day; listening to a walking Activation instead of music for 20 minutes on your way to work; doing at-home Pilates three times per week while watching TV; or investing $100 every month. With each passing day, week, or year, small habits like these would have compounded, gradually building momentum and propelling you toward remarkable achievements.

Compounding is so important to understand in the context of habits, good and bad. As you know, habits are simply small actions that we do consistently over time. When we develop positive habits, we're essentially harnessing the power of compounding in our favor. Each time we perform a positive habit, we're reinforcing that behavior and making it more likely that we'll do it again in the future.

For example, imagine you consistently eat unhealthy food and skip workouts. At first, it might not seem like a big deal – you might not notice any significant negative effects. But as these small actions accumulate, they can lead to serious health problems like obesity, diabetes, and cardiovascular diseases. Each unhealthy meal and missed workout might seem insignificant on its own, but over time, they can add up to a major health and body crisis.

Now think about the habit of procrastination. Initially, delaying tasks might not seem harmful. But consistently putting off important work will result in a poor self-image, missed opportunities, increased stress, and a backlog of tasks that becomes overwhelming. Over time, the habit of procrastination will severely impact your productivity and overall success, turning a small issue into a massive roadblock.

Seemingly small but negative financial habits will have a profound impact as well. Regularly overspending or accruing large amounts of debt might not have immediate consequences, but these actions will lead to significant problems over time, causing stress, financial insecurity, and the inability to achieve financial goals. My rule is that if it can't be paid for immediately, it shouldn't go on the credit card.

The same principle applies to mental and emotional habits. Consistently indulging in negative self-talk or pessimistic thinking will erode your self-esteem and self-image and potentially lead to chronic stress, anxiety, and depression. Over time, these negative thought patterns will become deeply ingrained, making it challenging to adopt a more positive Future Self mindset. If you constantly tell yourself, 'I can't do this,' you'll eventually believe it to the point where you stop trying altogether.

Being aware of our daily actions and making conscious choices to avoid negative habits will prevent these compounding effects and help us maintain a healthier, more balanced life. And get closer to our Future Selves! Remember, it's the little things that count. By being aware of and addressing these negative habits, you can stop them from snowballing into something much bigger and more difficult to manage.

A Guide to Making Better Decisions

Throughout our lives, we need to make a multitude of decisions, and if we don't have a well-thought-out plan of action, we're at risk of making hurried, impulsive choices. Or maybe you're the type who freezes in the face of decisions and ends up not making one at all. Wouldn't it be great if you felt empowered and confident in the decision-making process? Below is a simple framework for making decisions, both big and small, that are more aligned with your Future Self.

For big decisions, such as choosing a person to marry, buying a house, moving to a new country, starting a business, opening up to a family member about a serious issue, changing careers, getting divorced, having children (or adopting), investing money, retirement, or starting a fitness program, ask yourself the following questions:

- **What are my options?** Make a list of all the possibilities that are available to you.

- **What are the potential outcomes of each option?** Consider the short-term and long-term consequences of each option.

- **How will this decision affect me?** Assess the impact on your emotional and physical well-being.

- **How will this decision affect others?** Make sure the impact this decision has on others is in alignment with your core beliefs and values.

- **How does this decision align with my Future Self?** Envision your ideal Future Self. Will this decision support your path to becoming this person, no matter how small?

- **What does my intuition tell me about this decision?** Reflect on your gut feelings and emotional responses to making this choice. Does it feel expansive or limiting? Wise or foolish?

- **What does making this decision feel like in my body?** Close your eyes and ask yourself, *Do I feel my body tensing up, or is it at ease?* Is your body leaning in, saying yes? Or is it leaning away, signifying a no?

For small decisions, such as what time to wake up every day, what to eat, which route to take to work, which clothes to wear, which exercise to choose, what your daily routine will be, water intake, alcohol intake, cleaning your home, purchasing clothes and personal items, and daily time management, ask yourself a simplified version of the questions above: Consider how each choice aligns with your values, supports your well-being, and brings you closer to your ideal Future Self. Trust your intuition to guide you in making decisions, both big and small, that support a balanced and fulfilling life.

Finally, once you've made a decision, *feel at peace with it*. Know that everything happens for a reason, and whatever decision you make will ultimately be the right one because you made it.

Dealing with Uncertainty

While you're making a big decision, it's normal to feel uncertain. If you're not in a rush to make a particular decision, spend one day pretending that you've already made it. See how it feels. For example, if you're unsure if you should end a relationship, for one day, visualize yourself doing it, and see how it feels in your mind and body. What new options could open up for you if this decision was made? What regrets might you have? Are these reasonable thoughts, or fear-based ones that are clouding your judgment?

Another useful exercise for dealing with uncertainty is to separate the aspects of the decision about which you're uncertain into two lists: the things you can control and the things you can't control. Those in the 'can't control' list are where you first focus your energy – into acceptance. Acceptance doesn't mean you have to like this truth. It just means that you're aware it's out of your hands. Let it go. Next, look at the list of the things you 'can control' and write down the actions you can take in those situations. Remind yourself that you're equipped with free will to steer your future.

Once you've identified what's within your control, your choices become clearer. Let's say you're considering moving to Vermont because you felt a deep sense of happiness when you visited that state. To reduce uncertainty, start narrowing down key factors: What does the job market look like in Vermont? How does the real estate market compare to where you live now? Are housing prices affordable, and is it a good time to lock in a mortgage?

Which neighborhoods fit within your budget, and what are their crime rates? If staying connected to family and friends is important, how often will they realistically be able to visit, given the distance? Finally, are you prepared for Vermont's climate? By answering these types of questions, you can cut through uncertainty and reach a decision more confidently.

Aligning Decisions with Your Future Self

Are you a hesitater? If you were given an address that you hadn't been to before and had to drive there without a sat nav or a phone signal, forcing you to rely on gut instinct to decide on the route, would you feel stressed? What if a friend asked you to go to a concert but the $450 ticket is much more than you'd normally spend to see a band? In-the-moment decisions like these can test your nerves. But maybe it's time to see them as opportunities, especially when they're small decisions. Why? Because they give you consistent practice in choosing. In leading you into your future. They can build confidence that you're directing life, not letting life direct you.

Knowing what your values are and being able to connect to them in decision-making is also powerful in making quick decisions. Look at your values and you ask yourself, *Does this decision put me in alignment with my priorities?* If the answer's yes, then you're going to have more energy or a more soul-connected feeling that it's the right decision.

You can also ask yourself, *Does this decision move me toward my Future Self or away from my Future Self?* For me, this one question can get a lot of decisions made. For instance, if I was saving for a vacation and that $450 concert ticket would pull me away from reaching my goal, I'd easily see that the money would not be well spent.

Setting Priorities Consciously

What you decide to do with your time, money, and energy will dictate your future. The way you allocate these resources, and your attitude toward whether an investment is good or bad, reflects your true priorities and shapes the path you're on. Consider the examples below and what kind of Future Self these attitudes might lead to.

Upgrade to a new $1,000 iPhone:	Invest $1,000 in a personal growth course:
'I'll buy it the moment I receive my next paycheck.'	*'I don't have that kind of money!'*
Watch Netflix for an hour:	Read a business book for an hour:
'Time flies!'	*'I wish I had the time.'*
Spend $30 on Uber Eats:	Spend $30 on an Activations membership:
'A weekly habit.'	*'Way too expensive.'*

Every decision you make shapes your Future Self. You must consciously prioritize where you invest your time, money, and energy. If you do this, you can create a life that's aligned with your Future Self goals and aspirations. Remember, it's the cumulative effect of these small, daily choices that determines your ultimate path.

✦

We humans have a penchant for clean slates. Mondays, the start of a new year, or the first day of a month often feel like opportune times to start afresh; there's something intoxicating about the idea of reinventing ourselves. But the truth is that *every* moment you have is a new opportunity to reset, choose a different path, do the small, consistent daily actions necessary for real change, and become a better version of yourself. This shift in perspective is incredibly liberating. It allows you to focus on what you can do today to move closer to your goals.

Each small step you take, no matter how imperfect, brings you closer to your goals. Embrace the journey, with all its ups and downs, and appreciate the growth that comes from the process of continual improvement. This is the only way you'll ever find true success.

The allure of 'starting over' is strong, but don't let it blind you to the opportunities available right now. Seize those moments where you can step into your Future Self, and watch as these moments compound into real, lasting transformation.

ACTIVATION: BE YOUR FUTURE SELF NOW

It's time to live your future right now, using your mind and your body.

Begin to tune in to your Future Self energy, thoughts, beliefs and way of living.

Begin to feel what it feels like to live as your Future Self in this moment.

It is simply a conscious choice.

You can choose to be your Future Self right now.

All you need to do is give in. Open up to it.

Remember your Future Self is the true you. It's who you're meant to be.

So, remove the layers of what you're not and allow your potential to shine through.

Use visualization, use mental rehearsal in your mind as you move.

Feel and think like it's already your reality.

The thoughts you think, the beliefs you believe and how you think about yourself.

THIS is what creates your life.

So, choose to let go of old limiting thoughts and beliefs and step into your Future Self frequency. Begin to tune into your body.

FEEL that beautiful heart of yours. FEEL the energy inside and around you and begin opening up to every possibility that exists for you.

In this very moment, connect to your unlimited power.

Connect to your potential.

Visualize it with your body, feel what it feels like to be your Future Self now.

Act 'as if' in this exact moment!

Practice being your Future Self with your eyes open, feeling the frequency of your future with your whole body; physically stepping into a new reality.

Embodying your Future Self energy is simple.

It is easy.

It comes naturally to you.

How would your Future Self move in this moment?

What is your Future Self posture like?

How do they hold themselves?

What does it really feel like to live as your Future Self right now?

Transforming into who you want to be is simple. All you need to do is start living like it in this moment.

You must remember your potential in this moment, that unlimitedness inside of you... your power.

You are creating your future in the present moment.

So be an investor in your life. Invest in your future by being who you want to be right here, right now.

Start taking action as your Future Self would.

Start living like it in every facet of your life.

Surround yourself with people who align with this new you.

Begin acting like your Future Self – thinking like them, dressing like them, moving like them!

The more you do this, the more you tune in to who you want to be, the more you act as if and visualize you already being there... the faster this reality will unfold and eventually become your life.

So, take the shortcut.

Become who you want to be right now.

Commit to this, being who you need to be. Make a choice. In this very moment, choose to become them.

You only get to live this precious life once.

Now is the time.

Stop waiting, start FEELING and embodying your Future Self frequency!

Connect to it.

And finally become who you've always wanted to be.

You can use this script to create an Activation (*see instructions on pages 33–34*) or find it on the Activations app under Walking Activations.

PART III

MAINTAINING

This final section is about thriving in your new, effortlessly elevated reality – your Future Self – and learning to handle setbacks effectively as they arise. I'll show you why aiming for perfection isn't the goal, and you'll use my unique tools, the Bounce Back Rate and the Bounce Back archetypes, to better understand and improve the way you respond to challenges. I also offer practical strategies to keep you aligned with your Future Self, helping you stay on track and resilient in the face of adversity. By the end of this section, you'll have everything you need to maintain your growth and continue evolving, no matter what life throws your way.

CHAPTER 7

Perfection Is a Scam

Perfectionism can be one of the biggest obstacles to maintaining your new Future Self identity. While striving for an ideal life can feel like a motivator, it often becomes a barrier to genuine growth. The journey of connecting with and activating your Future Self isn't about getting everything right; it's about learning, adapting, and evolving.

From a young age, I was driven by the belief that success is synonymous with perfection – the perfect diet, a flawless morning routine, never procrastinating. These weren't just ideals but real expectations I set for myself, convinced that they were the only road to a life I could be proud of. However, maintaining this belief wasn't just exhausting, it was a recipe for guilt, anxiety, and shame each time I inevitably slipped up. It seemed to me that everyone who was happy was on the Forbes 400 list, and that all the role models in the glossy magazines I read had a secret formula for doing everything right. *What am I missing?* I wondered. *Why am I so bad at improving my life?*

But there's a twist to my story: I started to achieve real success and happiness in my life without having a single 'perfect' day. I've stumbled and fallen off track more times than I can remember, yet I've kept moving forward. And through this journey, I've realized that living a big, impactful life and experiencing rapid change doesn't ever require perfection. Instead, it requires resilience – the ability to *bounce back*.

As a recovering perfectionist, this realization was my greatest breakthrough. By simply adjusting my thoughts, beliefs, actions, and self-image and utilizing the tools and strategies I've outlined in Parts I and II of this book, I watched my life transform, step by step. I became my desired Future Self, radically improving my health and becoming a multimillionaire along the way.

And the key to my success wasn't trying to stay on track every minute of every day; it was returning to being my Future Self after veering off course. I began to focus on how *quickly* I could Bounce Back to acting and feeling like my Future Self. In 2016, recognizing that this was the most crucial metric for reaching my goals, I developed the Bounce Back Rate™. I'll teach you how to use this essential tool in the next chapter, but first, let's look at the scam that is perfection.

Progress Not Perfection

The most successful people in the world won't admit that they've never had a 'perfect' day in their life. Why? Because it would make them look weak. But the reality is that *perfection doesn't exist*. No one has ever managed to eat perfectly, think only positive thoughts, and stay in a blissful state for an extended period, all while avoiding gluten and sugar. Show me someone who claims that they never fall off track, and I'll show you a liar. In this chapter, I'll show you why the pursuit of perfection is not only counterproductive but also a massive barrier to your progress as you live as your Future Self.

We all have an image in our minds of what a perfect daily routine looks like: Getting out of bed at 5:00 a.m. and performing that perfect workout, followed by a day of seamless productivity and zero procrastination. Oh, did I mention only eating meals that perfectly follow your macros? And of course, no technology for one hour before bedtime.

Listen, I'm a strong advocate for discipline and pushing yourself to be better – it's an incredibly important part of becoming your Future Self and living the life you long for. Discipline is there when motivation is not, making it essential for maintaining momentum toward your goals. However, these immaculate and demanding daily routines, although intrinsically beneficial to our health and well-being, can be followed too rigidly and used to create perfectionistic goalposts. When this happens, it shifts our mindset to one of overwhelm instead of self-assured confidence.

Our modern culture of self-help and wellness has, in many ways, heightened this need to pursue an idealized version of how our life *should* be. The belief that it's possible to reach a place of absolute control and perfection, as compelling as it is, sets an unreachable standard that exhausts us, and leads to stagnation instead of motivation.

In other words, when you've promised yourself an hour-long yoga session after a long day at work, the couch will look more tempting than the yoga mat. Would a 20-minute yoga session be a step in the right direction, instead of doing no yoga at all? Not when overwhelm paralysis sets in, fueled by an unending wheel of striving for perfection, falling short, and then crashing into a sense of failure.

Overcoming the All-or-Nothing Mindset

This way of living is often built on a foundation of all-or-nothing thinking. The mindset in which anything less than perfection is seen as failure, doesn't leave any room for the natural ebb and flow of human energy and motivation. As a result, trying to initiate lasting change and improvement in our lives becomes a source of stress, leading us to burn out and feel shame about our 'lack of discipline.'

The all-or-nothing mindset holds us back more than propelling us forward, and it's hugely limiting because it sets us up for failure. No matter how disciplined you are, you're a human, not a robot. And perfection doesn't exist for humans. Our all-or-nothing thinking addiction is like flipping a switch. We either feel as if we're about to conquer the world, or as if we can't get anything right. It's what we encounter when we work on our goals, too, thinking that only a spotless outcome will do. Below are some common examples of all-or-nothing thinking:

- While on a strict diet, you indulge in a single cookie, which leads to finishing the entire pack, as the initial slip-up feels like a failure.

- During focused work time, a quick glance at your phone escalates into an hour lost to scrolling on Instagram, as the first distraction appears to ruin your entire day's productivity.

- Throughout the week, you meticulously budget every dollar, only to overspend during the weekend, believing that breaking your discipline even for a moment cancels out all previous progress.

This kind of self-limiting behavior only leads to shame, which then perpetuates the cycle of overwhelm paralysis.

Self-Sabotaging Behavior

Let's talk about one extreme aspect of the all-or-nothing mindset: self-sabotage. Self-sabotaging behavior is actions or thought patterns that interfere with our goals and well-being; it tends to be activated when we have an opportunity to empower ourselves, and overcoming it requires increasing our self-esteem, which means holding ourselves in high regard.

Our power to make lasting change is real, so why do we gravitate toward self-sabotage? Because becoming more empowered requires us to drop our unhealthy behaviors. Self-empowerment also removes our access to excuses as to why we aren't doing the best we can. We can't procrastinate once we know our potential. Yet we often don't want to deal with the consequences of living out our potential because we lack the self-esteem to follow through, which often activates the opposite emotion: self-loathing.

Self-esteem requires follow-through and consistency. You must be willing to lay aside your excuses for why you keep choosing self-sabotaging behaviors. Often, we give ourselves an out: 'I really shouldn't do this, but it's because of how I was raised.' We blame our parents, our teachers, our childhood, or anything but ourselves for why we make poor choices. But if we learn to take full responsibility for our behavior, we can no longer play the victim and blame an external source for our inability to move forward in life. When we know we're in a situation that represents an opportunity to become better and grow, it's paramount to engage our light instead of our shadow. Once this becomes our intuitive response, self-sabotaging behavior eventually stops.

Freezing in the Face of Perfection

The other thing that happens when you inevitably miss your target of perfection is that you *lose confidence*. Confidence is built through keeping promises to yourself, so it takes a big hit every time you fail. If you promise yourself that you'll be perfect and then mess up, your confidence falters, setting you back even further. When you're not confident, you become insecure. When you're insecure, you don't believe you're worthy of the big, beautiful life you deserve. When you feel unworthy, you stop trying to live as your ultimate Future Self.

Imagine standing on a diving board and staring down at the water as you prepare to make a 'perfect' dive; the more you think about achieving this, the harder it becomes to begin, and you become physically and mentally immobilized. This 'freeze' response is activated by the worry that you won't nail the dive perfectly, along with self-doubt, and fear of the unknown. In real life, your fear of not achieving perfection may mean you'll miss out on chances to grow, learn, and enjoy your life, all because you're scared to make a move unless it's the guaranteed 'right' move.

When we're under a ton of pressure to be perfect – whether self-imposed or societal – it feels like we're expected to achieve our goals flawlessly from the get-go, which is why we often freeze. It's not about being lazy or not trying hard enough; it's simply that the demand for perfection makes even starting something feel overwhelming. Starting imperfectly doesn't seem good enough, even though starting *somewhere* is exactly what we need to do.

The brain is an incredible organ, constantly processing a huge amount of information and making decisions that help us navigate our daily lives. When we encounter the expectation of perfection, the brain's fear center (known as the amygdala) kicks into high gear. This part of the brain is responsible for our fight, flight, or freeze response to threats. In the context of perfectionism, the amygdala perceives the risk of failure (or not being perfect) as a threat, triggering a freeze response. This is because, from a neurological standpoint, the potential emotional pain of failing is something the brain wants to avoid at all costs.[1]

Additionally, our prefrontal cortex – the area of the brain that governs planning, deciding, and socializing – really struggles with the pressure to hit perfection. It's in charge of juggling our good and bad choices. When the effects of not being perfect feel overwhelming, this part of our brain may very well shut down and refuse to take any action, to avoid potential pitfalls. When this happens, the prefrontal cortex essentially hits the pause button on our actions as it tries to shield us from facing those negative outcomes. What does this all mean? That our brains are programmed to initiate a freeze response when the pressure to be perfect becomes too intense.[2]

Understanding the neuroscience behind this process can empower us to break the cycle. Simply understanding that it's a natural brain response rather than a lack of discipline can help us be more compassionate with ourselves. This will help reduce the amygdala's response over time and strengthen the neural pathways in your brain that associate embracing imperfection with a positive outcome rather than a threat.

Stop Chasing Control

If you're a recovering perfectionist like me, you may well have a controlling side to you. Perfectionism often goes hand in hand with control issues. There's a myth that if everything were perfect, we'd be able to control all outcomes. Perfectionism is often disguised as the pursuit of excellence, but it's often based on a fear of vulnerability and unpredictability.

That being said, there's a spectrum to chasing control. Having a clear vision and a strong desire for things to unfold in a certain way is a good thing. It fuels your passion, makes you an ambitious person, and gives you direction. However, when this desire for a specific outcome becomes obsessive, it can blind you to possibilities outside of that fixed target.

Being a perfectionist and overly controlling
limits your ability to adapt and grow.

While it's commendable (and essential!) to have a vision, it's equally crucial to stay open to the limitless possibilities in life. Remember, the universe might have bigger plans for you than you have for yourself. It's the flow of life and the unexpected turns in our journey that lead us to where we're meant to be.

Creating your ultimate life comes down to your *embodiment of resilience*, not from the obsessive need to have every detail under constant control. The real world is unpredictable, and relying on your ability to recover from setbacks is far more effective than having a false sense of control through perfectionism; we'll talk more about resilience in the next chapter.

CASE STUDY: RACHEL

Let's look at a real-life example of someone who embarked on the process of letting go of control. Rachel, one of my podcast listeners, was a high achiever with a packed schedule, balancing her demanding job with a strict workout routine and an active but frustrating dating life. She believed that maintaining perfect control over every aspect of her life was the key to finding happiness. Yet, despite all her efforts, she felt exhausted and unfulfilled.

Rachel approached dating as if it were another task to master and held rigid expectations for herself and the men she met. But after yet another disappointing date, she finally asked herself, *What's the point of being so perfect if I'm not even happy?*

Rachel realized that her obsession with chasing control and perfection was standing in the way of her finding true love. So, she decided to let go. She stopped overanalyzing every interaction and let herself be more open and genuine. She started enjoying the process of getting to know someone rather than focusing on whether each date met her preconceived standards. This change in attitude made a profound difference.

One evening, she went on a date with a man who she would have previously dismissed as 'not perfect enough,' but found instead that he really saw and appreciated her true self. They connected over shared values and genuine laughter, and for the first time, Rachel felt that she wasn't just checking boxes, she was building something real.

By releasing her need for perfection and control, Rachel found her soulmate in the most unexpected way, realizing that love doesn't thrive under pressure; instead, it flourishes when you allow yourself to be vulnerable and authentic.

Choose Adaptability Over Perfectionism

Adaptability is the ability to shift, bend, and adjust to new conditions without being resentful, getting off track, or 'stuck.' It requires you to go beyond simply enduring something difficult and focus on thriving as you navigate your way through it. Perfectionism blocks our ability to be adaptable because, due to its rigid nature, it doesn't support flexibility. Another downside to perfectionism is that it holds us back from trying new things, even if those new things will help us achieve our goals faster.

Perfectionism permits us to view just one narrow, strict path ahead, while adaptability enables us to see the big picture, and pivot when necessary. This behavior lets us grow and learn, changing our plans when we need to, which is far better for personal and professional growth than just trying to do it 'one way' all the time. Being adaptable means that when things don't go as planned, or we're exposed to a better way, we can quickly change course and improve.

Being able to change and grow with whatever life throws at us leads to real, lasting success.

The business story of Stewart Butterfield, the Canadian entrepreneur who cofounded the team-based messaging software Slack, offers a perfect example of why adaptability is crucial for success. His original intention was to create a gaming platform, but it didn't take off; however, while working on this project, he and his team devised a chat tool for communicating with each other that worked very well. Instead of just sticking to his game plan, Butterfield saw something special in this chat tool, so he decided to switch gears and focus on improving it.

If Butterfield had stuck to his original gaming idea, the multibillion-dollar business Slack wouldn't exist. This shows how important it is to be open to change and ready to move in a new direction when you see a good opportunity, even if it's not what you first planned. Being overly perfectionist can limit our vision, making us oblivious to the potentially huge opportunities that life may throw our way. Life is unpredictable and boundless. You must open your mind, so you don't miss any opportunities.

CHAPTER 8

Know Your Bounce Back Rate

I n this chapter, I'm going to guide you through two simple yet highly effective tools I've created that will get you to where you want to be faster and more easily: The Bounce Back Rate™ and the Bounce Back archetypes. As you progress on your journey to becoming your Future Self and achieving the life you desire, it's inevitable that you'll encounter setbacks, obstacles, and moments of self-doubt. When these issues threaten to throw you off track, using these Bounce Back tools will help you quickly revert to the mindset and energy of your Future Self.

How the Bounce Back Rate Works

You can think of the Bounce Back Rate as a resilience meter with two indicators – awareness level and response time – which, when combined, show the *speed* and *efficiency* with which you recognize and respond to setbacks: this is your Bounce Back Rate. Identifying your current Bounce Back Rate and understanding what you can do to make it faster, can mean the difference between thriving and endlessly repeating the same mistakes that dig you further and further into a life you don't want to live.

Awareness Level

Your awareness level is the degree to which you're aware of what's going on within you and in how you respond to specific setbacks, such as procrastinating for too long or sleeping in too late to do your morning walk. The higher your awareness level, the better you'll be able to live as your Future Self and reach your goals. The lower your awareness level, the longer you'll be stuck in Old Self behaviors.

- **High**: You immediately recognize that a setback has occurred, allowing for swift action and minimal disruption.

- **Medium**: It takes a day or two for you to realize that you've strayed from your path, which delays your response slightly.

- **Low**: Only after a significant period (more than a week) or following external intervention do you recognize the setback.

Response Time

Your response time is how long it takes for you to act on getting back on track. Those who hesitate or procrastinate in response to setbacks generally don't achieve as much as those who act with confident precision. It's essential to note that it's virtually impossible to have a low awareness level paired with an immediate response time; awareness is a prerequisite for quick action.

- **Immediate**: You Bounce Back right away and change course.

- **Short**: You adjust your path after a day or two.

- **Long**: It takes several days or even weeks for you to Bounce Back and course correct.

✦

In this part of the book, I'll show you how to take targeted action to raise both your awareness level and your response time to achieve a faster Bounce Back Rate, which will ultimately align you more closely with your Future Self and help you achieve the results you truly desire.

When you develop a faster Bounce Back Rate, you're essentially saying, 'I won't let setbacks deter me for long.' Every moment you spend dwelling on a setback, wallowing in a victim mentality, or focusing on disappointment is a moment you're not moving toward your goals. The world's most successful people understand this intuitively. They've mastered the art of quick recovery, not just because they're resilient but because they know that time is of the essence.

Think about this: In the fast-paced world we live in, opportunities come and go quickly. If you're still ruminating over a past failure or setback, you might miss the next big chance knocking at your door. But if you've trained yourself to Bounce Back swiftly, you'll always be ready and primed to take advantage of new opportunities.

Over time, this ability gives you a huge advantage over others. You're not only facing challenges head-on, but you're also turning them into stepping stones that will take you closer to your dream life and your ultimate self. In the long term, a fast Bounce Back Rate doesn't just mean you recover quickly, it also means you're consistently in the right place at the right time, ready to make your next power move.

Bounce Back Rate Archetypes

I've devised seven Bounce Back Rate archetypes, which have corresponding Bounce Back Rates and key qualities and traits. These archetypes are intended to help you uncover the reason why your Bounce Back Rate may not be optimal right now, and to see what an optimal, faster, one looks like.

Find yourself in the definitions below but be aware that archetypal patterns are always evolving within us, so don't be discouraged if at first you identify with one that isn't always helpful.

The Responder

- **High awareness level**

- **Immediate response time**

- Pioneering attitude

- Visionary

- Action and confidence

This is the one to aim for! If you can embody the Responder, then you're in your Future Self energy. Responders have a need to leave the negative parts of their past behind and move on so they can explore a Future Self that meets their new expectations. They are flexible and able to adjust to changing circumstances. They elevate the energy around them, helping other people to achieve their best self too. While not perfect, they embody the confidence that's necessary for a fast Bounce Back Rate.

The Hesitater

- **High awareness level**

- **Short response time**

- Seeks validation before decision-making

- Overly cautious

- Risk-averse, leading to missed opportunities

This is the second-best archetype. The Hesitater often gets caught up in the world of 'what ifs' and 'maybes.' They are also self-doubters, even when they possess all the facts that they need to act. Hesitaters crave approval and connection but at times fear rejection and failure, which is why their response time is longer than that of the Responder. They tread lightly and take deliberate steps before acting because they fear making the wrong choice. Trusting their instincts would help improve their response time, leading to a faster Bounce Back Rate.

The Overthinker

- **High awareness level**

- **Long response time**

- Anxiety over action

- Analysis paralysis

- Perfectionism stalls progress

The Overthinker can spend hours researching things and tends to overanalyze every conversation; they also have a to-do list for their to-do list! Even though they quickly recognize what needs to be done, there is significant anxiety or hesitation about taking the necessary steps.

The Overthinker fears making the wrong choice, which leads to crippling procrastination. This archetype signals low self-esteem, feelings of unworthiness, and self-doubt, and activates the inner critic. The desire to wait for the 'perfect' moment or 'best' plan results in significant delays in responding to challenges, despite a clear understanding of what needs to be done. Overthinkers often get stuck in this loop over and over until they change their self-image. At the beginning of our journey to becoming our Future Self, most of us embody this archetype.

The Reactor

- Medium awareness level

- Immediate response time

- Acting before thinking

- 'Fire then aim' mentality

- Ability to self-correct

The Reactor will make decisions without first having all the necessary information. But when they realize that they've fallen off track, they kick into gear. Their Old Self habits are still ingrained, so they instinctively 'react' rather than gain a thorough awareness of the situation. Reactors forget who they want to be – their Future Self. Why? Because they have a need to please and 'do something' over doing what's best through rational, calm processes. When the Future Self is activated, this awareness increases, so keeping their vision clear and ever-present is a must!

The Delayer

- **Medium awareness level**
- **Short response time**
- Avoidance behaviors
- No sense of urgency
- Often defers to others

The Delayer, though somewhat aware, consistently postpones actions, decisions, or responses. Unlike the Hesitater, whose indecision stems from self-doubt, the Delayer may procrastinate because of fear of failure, lack of motivation, or feeling overwhelmed. They may delay responding to avoid potential mistakes and failures. When they realize they have gotten off track, which they always do, they still doubt themselves and slow their Bounce Back Rate.

The Self-Saboteur

- **Medium awareness**
- **Long response time**
- Delayed stress response = delayed action
- Unworthiness issues
- Frustration in personal growth

The Self-Saboteur activates every time there's an opportunity for empowerment, which causes them to make choices that block their success. While all the Bounce Back archetypes require a boost of self-esteem, the Self-Saboteur needs the heftiest dose! They truly feel unworthy of a good life and will destroy opportunities by failing to act and keeping their head in the sand. The more we know, the more we're held accountable for our choices, so they often don't want to know too much because it would lead to self-accountability and self-empowerment.

The Self-Saboteur battles voices in their head that generate negative emotions in everyday life situations and challenges. Saboteurs cause stress, anxiety, self-doubt, frustration, restlessness, and unhappiness. Only after repeated exposure to the same issue do these individuals begin to acknowledge and address it, leading to inconsistent outcomes. There's a sense of frustration or dissatisfaction due to recognizing issues but not dealing with them swiftly enough to make impactful changes.

The Victim

- **Low awareness**

- **Long response time (if any)**

- Powerlessness

- Dependency on others

- Blame is outward rather than inward

This is the lowest-ranking archetype because, unlike the Self-Saboteur, these people fail to take responsibility for their actions (or non-actions). Others are always to blame for why things don't work out. Feelings of helplessness, fear, vulnerability, entitlement (due to the 'poor me' mindset) are allowed to run rampant.

The Victim is also low on self-love and adaptability. They see themselves as victims of circumstance instead of agents of change. They give up their personal power because they don't even believe they have any. These people are often taken advantage of, and the road back to self-empowerment requires bravery and self-trust.

Staying Aligned with Your Future Self

Now let's connect the Bounce Back archetypes with the Bounce Back Rate so you can better understand how this system works. Your level of awareness and response time indicate how aligned you are with the self-image of your Future Self. Any misalignment often translates into missed opportunities and delayed reactions when challenges arise in your life, preventing you from taking the necessary steps toward your goals. For example, if you score low on the awareness level and long on the response time there's a high likelihood you don't have the self-image of someone who is experiencing the life you desire.

Now, here's where it gets interesting. If you find that you score high on the awareness level, noticing right away when things aren't going as planned, but then you drag your feet with a long response time before taking action, it's time to dig a bit deeper. What's holding you back? Often, it's a mix of a few internal battles. Maybe it's feeling unworthy deep down; or perhaps you're overanalyzing each setback, stuck in 'analysis paralysis.' It could be that perfectionism is holding you back, making you wait for that elusive 'right' moment to jump back in. Or perhaps you just need more time than others might to process emotions.

Understanding these nuances about yourself can unlock a huge shift in how effectively you respond to life's challenges, aligning you more closely with your Future Self and propelling you toward the life you envision. Tracking your Bounce Back Rate over time will also be essential to measure how you're improving, day by day.

A Quality Bounce Back

The Bounce Back Rate isn't *just* about speed; it's also about the *quality* of your Bounce Back response. A fast Bounce Back may give you immediate relief, but if it doesn't address the underlying issue, you might find yourself facing the same setback again. A quality Bounce Back means understanding the cause of the setback, learning from it, and moving forward with that knowledge. It's about rising up quickly and wisely, ensuring that you're setting yourself up for more success in the future! Just like any muscle, the more you exercise your ability to Bounce Back, the stronger and more resilient it becomes.

Be aware, too, that not all setbacks are created equal, and when you encounter more complex or severe ones – from physical and mental health issues to relationship difficulties, from job loss to personal debt, and from natural disasters to global pandemics – you should give yourself grace and time to heal before Bouncing Back. These are big life events that can derail anyone, even those who are the most dedicated to their Future Self. When faced with these challenges, your discipline is tested to the fullest, making the Bounce Back process more demanding.

The goal is progress. With progress comes confidence. With confidence comes enthusiasm. Those positive feelings create a cycle that fuels more abundance.

While we can't avoid life's bigger challenges – we'll always face struggles and disappointments – we can build a resilience that makes them less impactful over time. Remember, patience is going to get you there. Every time you Bounce Back, you're not just recovering, you're *evolving*.

Bounce Back Rate Hacks

Bridging the gap between recognizing you've fallen off track and effectively getting back on track can be challenging. Here are some high-level strategies to help:

- **Visualize:** Imagine yourself successfully overcoming obstacles and achieving your goals. This can make the path forward clearer and more attainable.

- **Trust your instincts:** Often, the first solution that comes to mind is the right one. Trusting your gut can streamline decision-making and help you take action more swiftly.

- **Take imperfect action:** Waiting for the perfect moment or solution can lead to analysis paralysis. Instead, focus on taking small, imperfect steps toward your goal. Progress, no matter how small, builds momentum.

- **Build a support system:** Sharing your goals with a friend, mentor, or coach can provide the external motivation and support needed to stay on track. Accountability partners can offer encouragement and help you stay committed to living as your Future Self (*see page 196*).

- **Journal daily:** Regularly writing about your thoughts, progress, and challenges helps maintain focus and self-awareness. Journaling can also uncover patterns and insights that aid you in navigating back to your path (*see page 191*).

Bounce Back Blockers

Bounce Back blockers are obstacles that hinder our ability to recover quickly from setbacks. They can manifest in various forms, often subtly influencing our behavior and mindset, and can drain our energy, sap our confidence, and prevent us from moving forward. Being aware of these blockers is crucial because they create invisible barriers that limit our potential and slow our progress. They can prevent us from taking advantage of opportunities, achieving our goals, becoming our Future Self, and living a fulfilling life. Below is a list of the most common Bounce Back blockers:

1. Overcommitment

2. Dwelling on past mistakes

3. Avoiding difficult conversations

4. Comparing ourselves to others

5. Ignoring boundaries

6. Delaying decisions

7. Constantly seeking external validation

8. Neglecting our personal development

9. Avoiding responsibility

10. Engaging in toxic relationships

11. Excessive complaining

12. Overindulging in distractions

13. Not prioritizing our self-care

14. Resisting feedback

15. Hesitating to set goals

16. Numbing out on social media/other technology

17. Addiction

18. Fear of failure

19. Lack of organization

20. Holding grudges

21. Chronic worrying

22. Poor time management

23. Perfectionism

24. Negative self-talk

25. Inconsistent routines

These blockers make it harder to Bounce Back when you stray off the path to becoming your Future Self, but it's up to you to actively work on changing them. Which of these blockers do you find yourself struggling with the most? Remember, you are 100 percent responsible for your life. By recognizing and actively working to overcome these blockers, you'll build up your resilience. Every small step you take to tackle them brings you closer to a more fulfilling and successful life.

Embracing the Bounce Back Rate

As you work to improve your Bounce Back Rate by using the exercises and tools throughout this book, you're not just adopting a new mindset. Thanks to neuroplasticity – which, as we discussed earlier, is the brain's capacity to change its structure and function throughout life in response to new experiences and knowledge – you're also creating new neural connections that reinforce resilience, persistence, and adaptability. The more you practice and internalize the Bounce Back Rate, the stronger these neural pathways become, making it easier to recover from setbacks and maintain a growth-oriented perspective.

What's fascinating is that these neural changes don't just impact your thought patterns; they also influence your behavior and emotions. As you consistently improve your Bounce Back Rate and develop a more resilient mindset, your actions and feelings begin to align with this new way of thinking. You'll find yourself recovering more quickly and confidently from setbacks and self-doubt, empowering you to face challenges head-on and continue your journey toward personal growth.

Note that this process of rewiring your brain applies to all aspects of personal development. Whenever you learn something new, overcome an obstacle, or push your limits, you're strengthening your brain's capacity for growth and adaptability. This capacity for change underscores the importance of lifelong learning and self-improvement in unlocking your full potential.

Embracing the Bounce Back Rate as a tool for resilience and adaptability is just one of many ways to harness the brain's capacity for change. As you continue to challenge yourself and expand your horizons, you're not just transforming your life, you're actively rewiring your brain for success. You'll begin to feel an unstoppable momentum building within you.

Setbacks will no longer hold you back; instead, they'll become opportunities for growth and learning. You'll develop an unshakable resilience, allowing you to Bounce Back faster and stronger each time. The bottom line? It's not about being perfect; it's about being fiercely and relentlessly persistent and resilient in the pursuit of personal growth and success. Embrace the Bounce Back Rate and watch as your life transforms before your eyes.

CHAPTER 9

Making Setbacks
Work for You

As you work toward becoming your new, true self – your
Future Self – you may experience setbacks that succeed in
derailing your progress and lead to failure and rejection. As you
become increasingly attuned to your Bounce Back Rate, you can
think more deeply about the way you respond to both setbacks
and failure. It's essential to reframe your perception of them and
recognize that they're an essential part of the journey to living
your most successful, fullest life.

Failure helps you to learn what works and what doesn't, offering
you the insights necessary to make better decisions. It's about
adapting and evolving as you head toward your ultimate goals.
Understanding that failure is an expected and manageable part
of your transformative journey means you can start to engage
with the possibilities and opportunities it holds.

I'm not afraid of failure, nor do I let it frustrate or overwhelm
me. Because every single time I fail, I know that I'm one step
closer to where I need to be. Failure teaches us so much. It
gives us character, wisdom, and a sense of purpose. And if I'm
not failing, I get concerned because it means I'm not taking

big enough actions and I'm playing it too safe. A little risk is necessary! Without taking big enough actions, we remain stagnant in life. Failure means we're moving, learning, and figuring out which direction is right for us.

Turning Failure into Success

Many of the world's most successful people have a trait in common: they're unafraid of failure. In fact, they embrace it. Read about any billionaire, and you'll discover that they keep going forward despite failure. They don't let it hold them back because they understand it's inevitable. They have the wisdom to know that failure is part of the process.

Consider Thomas Edison, the 19th-century American inventor. At school, his teachers told him he was 'too stupid to learn anything,' and later he was fired from his first two jobs for a lack of productivity. However, he went on to hold a world-record – 1,093 patents for his various inventions – and helped introduce the modern world of electricity. While developing his incandescent light bulb, he tested thousands of different materials to make the carbon filament before finding the right one. 'I have not failed,' he said, 'I've just found 10,000 ways that won't work.'

Then there's Oprah Winfrey, who was fired from her first TV job for being 'too emotionally invested in her stories.' She went on to build a media empire and today is one of the richest and most influential women in the world.

And let's not forget Whitney Wolfe Herd, the American entrepreneur who left the global online dating platform Tinder amid controversy and turned her setback into success by founding the rival app Bumble. She revolutionized the dating app scene by empowering women and became the youngest female CEO to take a company public. Her story shows how challenges can spark innovation and lead to industry-defining achievements.

These people, and thousands of others like them, demonstrate that failure is a step on the path to achieving greatness. The moment you realize this truth and embrace this mentality, you position yourself as a top achiever. Gradually, you'll get closer to your goals and ultimately achieve them. Embracing failure and welcoming it is the key.

Remember, everything happens for a reason. For example, if you've tried your absolute best to make a business idea work and it didn't, you've gained invaluable lessons. You've acquired wisdom you wouldn't have had otherwise, and you might even discover that this career path wasn't truly aligned with you. Learning when to close a chapter, even if it appears to be a failure, is one of the best business decisions you can make.

Turning failure into success is all about being able to pivot and listen to your gut instinct. We get so attached to certain things because of what we think the world will think of us if we give up. We need to remove the shame from our failures.

If you want to be a successful businessperson, you need to stop caring about what people think. If you want to live your most abundant, happiest life, you're going to have to try many different things to see what makes you truly happy and successful. You can't expect to get it right on the first try. If it were that easy, everyone would be doing it.

*The universe rewards resilience. If you
fail and quickly get back up to try
something else, you're much more
likely to achieve the life you desire.*

If you want to stand out and be one of the top achievers, you must start embracing failure and reprogramming how you think about it. Most people give up after one failure or are too scared to even try. They let fear and uncertainty paralyze them. But when you understand that failure is just a step on the path to living your ultimate life, you'll see that it's a good sign. It means you're gaining wisdom and growing.

It's all about perception. There are people who fail massively in business and then never try again. But what if their third attempt would have made them a billionaire? Being open to failure makes you resilient. Embracing failure when it arrives allows you to get back up and keep going without emotional damage. This is so important. I'm sure you can think of at least one person in your life who lives small because of their fear of failure. And you can probably think of someone else, whether you know them personally or have seen them in the media, who isn't scared of failure and has created a big life for themselves.

Dealing with Rejection

I learned the term 'no means next' in Jack Canfield's book *The Success Principles*. Canfield says that every 'no' you encounter should be seen as an indication to move on to the next opportunity.[1] Returning to Thomas Edison as an example here, his journey as an inventor was marked by failed attempts and rejections yet he persisted. Rejection means you're actively putting yourself out there, and every 'no' brings you closer to that awaited 'yes.'

We've all been rejected at some point in our lives, whether by a potential romantic partner, in our careers, or even in simple day-to-day moments. If you adopt the mindset that failure and rejection are simply *redirections* to something better, you'll live a much happier life.

Remember the Reticular Activating System (RAS) we spoke about earlier? Training your RAS to focus on what truly matters to you will also make you more resilient because being rejected or failing won't seem like such a big deal. You need that resilience and a fast Bounce Back Rate to succeed. Rejection lets us reevaluate and refine our desires, pushing us closer to our true goals and ultimate self.

> *Each rejection and setback is not a dead end but a detour directing you to a path that aligns better with your true purpose and potential.*

You can also use the energy from rejection to propel you forward. This is a strategy used by some of the most successful people in the world, who use rejection as their motivation, trusting the process and using it as fuel. You cannot be sad about failing or being rejected and then expect to win. Negative emotions will likely prevent you from taking as much action as you could. You need to embrace rejection. When you're rejected, it means that the person, place, or thing wasn't meant for you. There's absolutely zero point in wasting mental energy on what could have been when you could be channeling that same energy into what's next and potentially better.

Trust the Unfolding of Your Life

As I mentioned earlier, we often become fixated on a certain vision and forget to be flexible and open. Life doesn't always go to plan, and that's part of its beauty. If we knew exactly what we were going to get, life would be boring. You need to be open to new experiences and opportunities, even the misaligned ones. Work toward your goals, focus on them, take the necessary actions, and embody the self-image you want. However, also be open to receiving something different, knowing that your intuition will guide you in the right direction.

If you listen to your intuition and mix it with a sense of peace and the understanding that rejection is the universe's way of saying there's something greater waiting for you on the other side, you'll create a potent combination for success. Picture living your life with the belief that everything is unfolding exactly as it should. This new mindset will be undeniably transformative for you. Here are some examples of how it can play out in various scenarios:

- **Your long-term partner broke up with you.** It was devastating at the time, but you would have never met the real love of your life six months later if it hadn't happened.

- **You didn't get the 'dream' job** after countless interviews and hours spent on a take-home project. But if you'd gotten the job, you would have never started that side hustle that turned into a successful business that fulfills you.

- **You missed out on a prestigious college admission,** which made you feel crushed and lost. However, you ended up attending a different university, where you met a mentor who inspired you to pursue a career path you'd never considered before, leading to unexpected success and fulfillment.

- **Your startup failed after years of hard work**, leaving you in financial trouble and doubting your abilities. But this failure taught you invaluable lessons and connected you with a community of like-minded entrepreneurs. This network eventually led to your role in a groundbreaking tech company that changed an industry.

- **You were passed over for a promotion** you worked tirelessly for, only to find a new job opportunity that aligned even better with your values and career goals. This new role brought you more success, and more happiness!

Hindsight helps us to see things with clarity. If you simply look for proof that the universe has your best interests at heart, you'll find it. When you find it, you'll trust the universe more. The next time you face a setback, remember that it's just a setup for something greater. Trust that the universe has big plans for you. Keep your faith and lean in.

Choose how you want to live your life. Decide the baseline of how you want to feel every day. Our time on this Earth is limited. Understanding this will help you realize that there's no time to waste. You must start thinking in a new way to get different results and, more importantly, to start enjoying your life more. Even if you don't achieve your goals immediately, you can still lead a more peaceful, happy, and contented life by feeling supported by your higher self, God, Mother Nature – whatever term resonates with you. Know that you're supported and have survived up to this point, despite failures and rejections.

This is the belief system of your Future Self. But guess what? Your Future Self will *still* face failure and rejection. You need to envision your Future Self as a real person. How do they respond when faced with rejection or failure? Think about that, journal about it, and understand that your Future Self's response will dictate your future life. Your Future Self has a fast Bounce Back Rate, and they are resilient. You know it. Your Future Self knows it. Remember, to foster resilience in the face of rejection and failure, you must believe that this is happening for a reason. Trust that you're being divinely guided to where you need to be. Embrace this belief system, and you'll not only find peace but also enormous success.

Your past doesn't define you; your ability to adapt, learn, and push forward does. Embrace failure, learn from it, and just know that the universe rewards people who keep going. By embracing this way of thinking, you set the stage for a life of fulfillment, achievement, and embodying your Future Self energy. Keep pushing forward and remember that each failure brings you one step closer to your goals.

CHAPTER 10

Your Future Self Maintenance Plan

In this final chapter, I offer several strategies to help you continually enhance your Bounce Back Rate and stay committed to actions that align with your goals, bringing you closer to your Future Self and the life you desire.

Establish a Positive Morning Routine

Having a strong morning routine is extremely important. It's a micro habit – a small, achievable behavior that you build up over long periods of time – that influences all your other habits. The power of a good morning routine lies in its ability to set the tone for the rest of your day, paving the way for a fast Bounce Back Rate and a series of actions aligned with your Future Self.

You become extraordinarily self-confident by repeatedly doing things that make you better, by pushing yourself to your limits, and by actually completing the tasks you promised yourself you'd do. Establishing a strong morning routine will help you reach your big goals. It will be the catalyst for much of your success. Take control of your mornings, and you'll take control of the outcome of your life.

I strongly suggest you try getting out of bed at least one hour earlier than you usually do and experience the beautiful calmness and clarity of your surroundings before the rest of the world wakes up. There's something transformative about getting up early. You're already one step ahead of everyone else, taking control of your day from the very moment it starts, and this peaceful time can be incredibly enriching. It's not just about waking up early; it's about using this time effectively to align yourself with your Future Self.

This early start does wonders for your self-image, too. Your subconscious starts to view you as the type of person who goes the extra mile, who trains their willpower muscle every single day so that it's strong when you need it most. This is when your deepest creative powers make themselves present and you get into what's known in positive psychology as 'flow' or more colloquially as 'being in the zone.'

Ideas for Your Routine

I don't want to be too prescriptive about what you should include in your morning routine, because it's truly different for every one of us, and it depends on our stage in life. However, there are two tools that I highly recommend you use: journaling (more on this coming up) and listening to an Activation or meditation. Here are some other things that could feature in your morning routine:

- Planning your upcoming workday in your diary

- Reading a chapter of an inspiring book

- Doing some exercise

- Taking a walk outdoors

- Completing a 'power hour' of focused work

It doesn't need to be complicated. This is simply time for you to connect with your Future Self and align with your goals. There are so many morning routines you could choose from. You could try Robin Sharma's 20-20-20 method, which involves dividing the first hour of our day into three 20-minute blocks; the first 20 minutes should be filled with exercise, the next 20 with reflecting (journaling, meditating, or activating), and the last with growing (reading or learning something new). Or you could design a routine that speaks to you personally. The key is to ensure that it's effective at changing your state and that it aligns you with your Future Self.

Sharma's book *The 5am Club* had a deep influence on my life about five years ago. He's an extraordinary individual and now, I'm lucky to say, a friend. I highly recommend his work, and this particular title is a special one to read if you're in a very ambitious time in your life. I'd be lying if I said I still wake up at 5:00 a.m. every day, but I do sprints in phases, depending on my goals and targets.

As I write this book, I'm in a phase of stepping into my feminine energy, slowing down after a decade of pushing myself to my limits. I'm a big believer in doing different things in different phases of our life. I needed to be in that intense, focused, and in-my-hustle era up until this new phase. And now, I'm trying a new way of living for a while. I want you to choose whatever phase resonates with you. If you haven't yet achieved a level of success you're satisfied with, go intense mode. I'm all for it, and I'll do it again in another phase of my life.

Treat Yourself with Love

Whichever phase you're in, get out of bed as early as you can, so you're not in a rush as you start the day. Make yourself a beautiful, nourishing breakfast. Put your phone away and romanticize your routine. I love making it a whole moment. I make my coffee, put on some music, light a candle, and take out my journal. If it's winter, I might light a fire in my fireplace. I like to get cozy, wearing a nice set of pajamas or some cashmere. Have you heard of 'hygge,' a Scandinavian concept that embodies coziness, comfort, and contentment? It's about creating a warm atmosphere and enjoying the good things in life. Imagine sitting by a crackling fire, wrapped in a soft blanket, with a hot cup of coffee in hand. This is hygge. It's about savoring small moments, finding joy in simple things, and making your environment comforting and inviting. By incorporating hygge into your morning routine, you set a peaceful and positive tone for your day.

How you do one thing is how you do everything. Start treating yourself with so much love. Romanticize your life, one little moment at a time. If you're going through your day stressed and rushed, your entire life will be stressed and rushed. Remember that.

Staying Aligned

The most important part of any morning routine is reminding yourself of your Future Self and your goals. It's crucial you keep these things top-of-mind. As motivated as you may be right now, in this moment, to change, you need to be realistic. Your mood will shift, and you'll forget this feeling of inspiration inside of you if you don't remind yourself of it on a regular basis. How many times have you set a goal, only to have it never be

met? What really happened? It was likely because you simply...
forgot about it. Or got distracted. And you didn't stay primed
in terms of motivation to keep doing what needed to get done,
to reach that goal. Remember:

Your mornings create your days.

Your days create your weeks.

Your weeks create your months.

Your months create your years.

Your years create your life.

This is why a morning routine is so important. This daily habit
will help remind you of who you want to be. The more you act
as if and embody the self-image and energy of who you want to
be (your Future Self), the closer you are to actually living that
life and achieving those goals.

Journaling

Journaling is a practice that's almost always in my morning
routine, whichever life phase I am in. Keep a daily or weekly
Future Self journal to track moments when you went off-course
and the time it took to Bounce Back. This helps tremendously
in recognizing common triggers.

Regular self-reflection is crucial for achieving your goals and
becoming your Future Self. A study at Dominican University in
California found that we're 42 percent more likely to remember
and follow through on our goals when we write them down.[1]
An article in *Forbes* goes further, explaining that 'writing goals
on paper happens on two levels: external storage and encoding.'
With external storage you're literally storing the information

about your goal in an accessible location (i.e. a piece of paper) to review at any time. Whereas 'encoding is the biological process by which the things we perceive travel to our brain... where they are analyzed.' Writing simply improves the encoding process and makes it easier to remember what you're actively trying to improve and change in your life.[2]

Taking time to consider your actions and progress helps you understand what works and what doesn't. Reflect on how you did today, yesterday, and throughout the week. Assess your successes and challenges and recognize patterns in your behavior and outcomes. Imagine how incredible it would be if next week went exactly as you'd envisioned it. Visualize your ideal week – each day filled with productivity, feeling amazing, and progress toward your goals – and then journal on it. This exercise keeps your objectives at the forefront of your mind and fuels your motivation and commitment to continuous improvement.

By regularly reflecting on your actions and envisioning your desired future, you align your daily habits with your long-term aspirations. This helps you stay focused, make better decisions, and maintain the momentum needed to transform your dreams into reality.

One of my favorite daily journaling sessions was created by Dr. Nicole LePera, the Holistic Psychologist; it features the following prompts:[3]

- My daily affirmation:

- I'm grateful for:

- The person I'm becoming will experience more:

- I have an opportunity to be my Future Self today when I:

- When I think about who I'm becoming I feel:

Sometimes when I have too much on my mind and I need to clear my thoughts and regain focus, I'll do a 'brain dump.' This is essentially just word vomiting onto a blank page in your journal as you unload the contents of your brain. Another great journaling practice is writing a letter from your Future Self. To do this, get into the state of being your Future Self and write yourself a heartfelt letter that dives into the life you now finally live. You can talk about how worth it the journey was, what it feels like being on the 'other side,' and so on. Read this a few times per week to remind yourself of what you're heading toward. It's incredibly moving, emotional, and motivating.

Communicate with Your Future Self

Why is journaling so effective? As we discussed earlier, it isn't just some woo woo practice; it's a science-backed mechanism. The very act of putting pen to paper stimulates the brain uniquely, aiding in processing and even reframing our experiences. Research consistently indicates that those who commit to journaling enjoy enhanced mental clarity, reduced stress, and even elevated physical health.[4] It's accessible, simple, and doesn't demand perfection.

Just set aside a little time regularly to reflect on your progress, understand yourself better, and design your desired future. Your entries can be rough and raw – they're for your eyes only. This is one of the best habits to adopt in your journey to creating an exceptional life.

When you write, you're communicating with yourself, getting clarity on how you feel and where you want to be. You can write as if you're having a conversation with your Future Self; you can tap into energy of abundance by listing out all the things you're grateful for in your life; you can plan your day/week/month/year and set out all the beautiful possibilities of your life. With every line, you're actively taking steps to mold your life, to understand its complexities, and to design your path. It's an intimate dance between your Old Self and Future Self.

Another powerful thing about journaling is its ability to keep you anchored to a topic, allowing deep introspection and exploration and the opportunity to dig in and fully experience your thoughts and desires. If we rely only on thinking, our mind naturally moves to the next thought, often before we're done ruminating on the main thing we're focusing on. While our thoughts can be fleeting, pulling us from one idea to the next, writing offers clarity, depth, and sustained focus. Gratitude journaling in particular puts you in a state of receivership for your desires.

So, try out the journaling techniques I've suggested here. Remember, the goal isn't perfection. Even if you only write three lines, try to make it a daily habit. I truly believe it will help you tremendously, making you feel more motivated, aligned with your Future Self, and inspired to take the right action.

Future Self Declarations

A morning routine is a brain-priming routine that helps you get into the state you desire. Another brain-priming tool is Future Self declarations – a bullet point list of everything that you're currently being and doing to ensure you'll achieve the successful life you desire. Here are some of my own declarations, which you can draw on to create your own.

- I'm extremely powerful. I achieve all the things I desire in my life.

- When I encounter my Old Self, I speak to her as my Future Self – with love, compassion, and decisiveness.

- I'm the kind of person who makes a lot of money, effortlessly. It's just who I am.

- I'm the kind of person who has an incredibly healthy and fit body.

- I'm the kind of person who has wonderful relationships with my family and friends.

- I'm the kind of person who speaks with innate confidence, clarity, power, and kindness.

I suggest that you read your Future Self declarations in the morning, as part of your routine, or before bed. It goes back to reminding yourself daily. Constantly. Make it part of your DNA. Motivation, drive, success, focus, clarity.

Stay Committed to Your Future Self

Incorporating the following practices and tools into your daily life can further boost your journey toward becoming your Future Self and maintaining this new life. By adopting them, you'll set yourself up for ongoing growth and positive change.

Use Technology to Your Advantage

Set Future Self notifications – reminders or alarms on your phone throughout the day to prompt moments of self-reflection and assess where you stand with your goals. The power of being regularly prompted is that it can keep you aligned with your intentions, helping you stay on top of your progress. These gentle nudges will serve as check-ins with your Future Self, encouraging you to adjust your actions and mindset in real-time.

Remind yourself of who you want to be by placing affirmations or your Future Self declarations on your phone's lock screen. You can easily do this by writing them in the Notes app, taking a screenshot, and setting it as your lock screen background. Every time you check your phone, you'll be reminded of your commitment to your Future Self, reinforcing your goals and maintaining a positive, goal-oriented mindset.

Seek Accountability

Find an accountability partner or group. Share your goals with someone who can hold you accountable. This relationship isn't just about tracking progress; it's about creating a supportive environment where you can reach out for encouragement when your motivation wanes. An accountability buddy or group can offer invaluable support, whether it's through weekly check-in calls, sharing challenges and successes, or providing a much-needed pep talk.

You could give this book to a friend and embark on the journey of becoming your future selves together. By reading the same material and applying the same principles, you could motivate one another and make the transformation more engaging and less daunting. Together, you become a strong mutual support system, helping you stay focused on your respective goals.

Celebrate Every Bounce Back

Make this a habit, regardless of how small the progress may seem. Acknowledging your resilience strengthens your Bounce Back Rate, encouraging a positive mindset and reinforcing the habit of seeing setbacks as opportunities for growth. By celebrating these moments, you train your mind to perceive every Bounce Back as a step forward, building confidence and a stronger commitment to your Future Self.

Think About Death and Fear Regret

On a more sobering note, sometimes the most powerful motivator to stay committed to your Future Self is to think of the stark reality of death and regret. At the beginning of this book, I shared my deepest fear – waking up one day in my old age and confronting the question, 'Who could I have been?' I believe this thought resonates with you as well. It's a fear that can shake you to your core because it speaks to the universal human experience of unrealized potential.

When you reach the end of your life, 99 percent of your regrets will likely be about the things you didn't do – the risks you didn't take, the words you didn't say, and the dreams you didn't chase. We often hold ourselves back, trapped by fear or uncertainty. But consider the cost of inaction. The regret of not trying, of not reaching out, of not stepping forward, is a very heavy burden to carry. I don't know about you, but I'd rather face the sting of failure than live with the regret of not having tried at all.

Part III of the book has laid out practical strategies for maintaining your Future Self – letting go of perfectionism, utilizing your Bounce Back Rate, optimizing your morning routine, journaling, surrounding yourself with support, and celebrating every step forward, no matter how small. But beneath all these tools is a deeper call to action: To live boldly and intentionally, knowing that our time is finite. When you embrace this truth, the fears that hold you back begin to shrink in comparison to the regret you might feel later.

So, let this be your reminder. Every day is a new chance to move closer to the life you truly want. Don't let fear or doubt keep you from becoming the person you are meant to be. Instead, think about the person you want to become, the stories you want to tell, and the legacy you want to leave behind.

ACTIVATION: BOUNCE BACK + MAINTAIN YOUR FUTURE SELF ENERGY

Remember this: You are fully in control of how you're showing up in your life.

You can maintain your Future Self energy on any average day.

Simply focus on the progress that you are making in any given moment.

Don't focus on perfection, and don't beat yourself up if you fall off track or make a mistake.

This is only going to hold you back further from your Future Self reality.

The trick is to focus on your Bounce Back Rate and measure that more than anything else.

This is the secret to success.

It's not about being perfect – it's about how quickly you can Bounce Back to being your best self again.

This is having a quick Bounce Back Rate – focusing on your response time. So right now, Bounce Back.

In this moment, practice Bouncing Back.

You must get intimately familiar with the feeling of going from your Old Self to your Future Self, because this is going to happen multiple times a day, as it does to everyone.

Perfection doesn't exist. The people who win are the ones with a quick Bounce Back Rate.

The ones who achieve their Future Self life, they know the things that hold them back.

They know that perfectionism, and fearing failure and rejection, would only keep them small.

So do it. You know your Future Self would.

Create a morning routine.

Stick to it.

Journal and self-reflect every day.

Carve out time in your busy schedule to just be.

Connect with your intuition.

Connect with your Future Self.

Allow yourself to be undistracted and trust the flow of your life.

Know that you are being divinely led to the life that you're meant to live.

Feel love and compassion for every version of yourself.

And when you fall off track, just remember that you are always one decision away from Bouncing Back and feeling like your best self again.

You're here to stay committed to your Future Self.

You know the things that hold you back.

And you know that you're always one decision away.

You have one life.

Now go out and live it.

✦

You can use this script to create an Activation (*see instructions on pages 33–34*) or find it on the Activations app under Pep Talks.

Conclusion:
You Can Have It All

U ltimately, the people who reach their goals, who ascend to the highest levels of success, are those who want it badly enough. So, ask yourself: *How badly do you want it?*

Life is not a dress rehearsal. You have one shot, one fleeting moment to make your mark. So, you must continually ask yourself if your actions, your choices, your daily habits are aligned with the life you truly desire. If you don't chase what sets your soul on fire, it will always remain just out of reach. If you don't invest your time and energy with fierce determination, the results will never materialize. No one will do it for you.

This journey is yours and yours alone to navigate, to fight for, and to conquer. And therein lies its beauty – the unparalleled thrill of knowing that you've built your destiny with your own two hands.

To strive for something with every ounce of your being, to push your limits and test the boundaries of what you believe is possible, is a rare gift. It's a path that few choose, a journey that requires courage, persistence, and a strong 'why.' But for those who dare to embark on this path, who dare to give their all, there awaits a reward beyond measure: a life that's full, rich, and deeply felt.

These are the people who don't just exist, they thrive. They're the ones who feel everything – the joy, the pain, the achievement, and the struggle. They're the ones who look at the world with a sparkle in their eyes, filled with a confidence that comes from knowing that they're living up to their fullest potential, living as their Future Self.

This feeling of operating at your highest level, of pushing yourself beyond your comfort zone, is the most intoxicating experience you'll ever have. It brings a sense of euphoria that can't be bought or bottled. Even if you've tasted it only briefly, you'll know its power. When you're driven by passion, when you act with unwavering commitment and pour your whole heart into your pursuits, that's when life's true magic unfolds. That's when you feel most alive.

This feeling isn't elusive; it's not something you have to search for in the dark corners of the world. It's been within you all along, waiting for you to recognize your own power and Future Self potential. The moment you believe in yourself, the moment you commit to living fully and fearlessly, is the moment you unlock the door to the life you always deeply knew you were meant to live.

Now, you stand at a crossroads. You have a choice to make. You can close this book, put it on a shelf, and let its words fade from memory. You might appreciate the temporary burst of motivation it provided, but let your self-doubt drown out its message. You can choose to stay in the comfort of familiarity, to listen to the voices that tell you to play it safe, to settle for a life that's just okay. And yes, you might lead a comfortable existence, love and be loved, and eventually be remembered by a few who were close to you. But if you choose this path, you might miss out on the deeper fulfillment and joy that comes from truly living your potential, leaving behind not just a name but a legacy of love, human potential, and a life well-lived.

Or you can choose a different path. You can choose to listen to that inner voice that whispers of greatness. You can decide, right here and now, to raise your standards, to embark on a journey of self-discovery and relentless self-improvement. You can dive into books that challenge and inspire you, cultivate habits that empower you, and surround yourself with people who lift you higher. You can spend time in quiet reflection, exploring your deepest dreams and desires, and pursue what sets your heart on fire. In doing so, you'll find a passion for learning, a thirst for growth, and a love for life that most people never know.

Yes, there will be setbacks. Yes, there will be days when doubt creeps in and motivation wanes. But you will rise above. You will remember who you are and what you're capable of. You will keep going, because you know that the greatest journey you can take is the one toward your best self.

This is your life. Your story. And you have the power to write it any way you choose. If wealth is your goal, believe in your ability to create abundance. If impact is what you seek, know that your words, your actions, your very presence can change lives. Find joy in every experience, in every challenge, and watch as the world transforms before your eyes. Fully embrace the intimate, beautiful journey of becoming your Future Self. Live a life so full and vibrant that the impact of your actions ripples through the lives of those you've touched.

You have one life, *and it's happening right now*. Don't waste a single moment waiting for the 'right time' or the 'perfect opportunity.' Life is short, and every day is a gift that won't come again. Don't settle for anything less than becoming the person you're truly meant to be. Take the leap, make the necessary changes, and step boldly into your future.

Your Future Self is waiting – don't keep them any longer.

References

Chapter 2: Be Your Future Self Now

1. Dispenza, J. (2014), *You Are the Placebo: Making Your Mind Matter*. London: Hay House

2. Connor-Savarda, B-N. (2023), 'The Science Behind Emotional Energy: Exploring the Vibrations of Our Emotional World', *Emotional Intelligence Magazine*: www.ei-magazine.com/post/the-science-behind-emotional-energy-exploring-the-vibrations-of-our-emotional-world [Accessed 26 September 2024]

3. Dispenza, J. (2017), *Becoming Supernatural: How Common People are Doing the Uncommon*. Carlsbad: Hay House

4. Quest, P. (2002), 'Auras and Chakras', The International Center for Reiki Training: www.reiki.org/articles/auras-and-chakras [Accessed 26 September 2024]

5. Church, D. (2018), *Mind to Matter: The Astonishing Science of How Your Brain Creates Reality*. Carlsbad: Hay House

6. HeartMath Institute, 'Exploring the Role of the Heart in Human Performance': www.heartmath.org/research/science-of-the-heart/energetic-communication/ [Accessed 27 September 2024]

7. *Ibid*

8. Chahine, L., Kanazi, G. (2007), 'Phantom limb syndrome: a review', *Middle East J Anaesthesiol*, 19(2): 345–55.

9. Hubacher, J. (2015), 'The phantom leaf effect: a replication, part 1', *J Altern Complement Med*, 21(2): 83–90.

10. McCraty, R., et al. (2009), 'The Coherent Heart: Heart–Brain Interactions, Psychophysiological Coherence, and the Emergence of System-Wide Order', *Integral Review*, 5(2)

11. Emoto, M. (2004), *The Hidden Messages in Water*. Emeryville: Beyond Words Pub

12. Cramer, J.G. (1986), 'The transactional interpretation of quantum mechanics', *Reviews of Modern Physics*, 58(3)

13. Panksepp, J. (2010), 'Affective neuroscience of the emotional BrainMind: evolutionary perspectives and implications for understanding depression', *Dialogues Clin Neurosci*, 12(4): 533–45.

Chapter 3: Change your Self-Image, Change Your Life

1. Maltz, M. (1960/1989), *Psycho-Cybernetics*. New York: Simon & Schuster

Chapter 4: Your Beliefs, Thoughts, and Emotions

1. Mylett, E. (2019), 'Control Your Identity Control Your Life', *The Ed Mylett Show*: www.edmylett.com/podcast/this-advice-will-change-your-life [Accessed 27 September 2024]

2. *Ibid*

3. *Ibid*

4. Dixon Murray, T. (2016), 'Why do 70 percent of lottery winners end up bankrupt?': https://www.cleveland.com/business/2016/01/why_do_70_percent_of_lottery_w.html [Accessed 26 September 2024]

5. Marshall, M. (2016), 'A placebo can work even when you know it's a placebo', Harvard Health Publishing: www.health.harvard.edu/blog/placebo-can-work-even-know-placebo-201607079926 [Accessed 26 September 2024]

6. Orth, U. and Robins, R.W. (2022), 'Is high self-esteem beneficial? Revisiting a classic question', *Am Psychol*, 77(1): 5–17.

7. Olson, M. (2021), 'Study provides deep dive into the neuroscience of placebo effects': https://home.dartmouth.edu/news/2021/03/study-provides-deep-dive-neuroscience-placebo-effects [Accessed 26 September 2024]

8. Ranganathan, V.K., et al. (2003), 'From mental power to muscle power – gaining strength by using the mind', *Neuropsychologia*, 42(7): 944–56.

9. Feinberg, C. (2010), 'On "the psychology of possibility"', *Harvard Magazine*: www.harvardmagazine.com/2010/08/the-mindfulness-chronicles [Accessed 26 September 2024]

10. Dispenza, J. (2019), 'Becoming Divine': https://drjoedispenza.com/dr-joes-blog/becoming-divine [Accessed 27 September 2024]

11. Trauma Research UK, 'What is the RAS?': https://traumaresearchuk.org/ras-reticular-activating-system/ [Accessed 27 September 2024]

12. *Ibid*

13. Ponurska, M. (2023), 'Think it, Achieve It: The neuroscience behind mental rehearsal', Medium: https://medium.com/@mponurska/think-it-achieve-it-the-neuroscience-behind-mental-rehearsal-cb2ad4a4de70 [Accessed 27 September 2024]

14. Bangert, M. (2006) 'Brain activation during piano playing', in Altenmüller, E., Wiesendanger, M., and Kesselring J. (eds), *Music, Motor Control and the Brain*. Oxford: Oxford University Press, pp.173–188.

15. Di Corrado, D., et al. (2020), 'Mental Imagery Skills in Competitive Young Athletes and Non-athletes', *Frontiers in Psychology*, 11: 633.

16. Phan, T. (2016), 'The impact of visualization on problem-solving performance', *Journal of Applied Psychology*, 101(3): 348–362.

17. Dossey, L. (2014), *One Mind: How Our Individual Mind Is Part of a Greater Consciousness and Why It Matters*. Carlsbad: Hay House

18. Di Corrado, D., et al. (2020), 'Mental Imagery Skills in Competitive Young Athletes and Non-athletes', *Frontiers in Psychology*, 11: 633.

19. Sauer-Zavala S. (2024), 'Personality Change Is Possible', *Psychology Today*: https://www.psychologytoday.com/us/blog/self-made/202402/personality-change-is-possible [Accessed 25 October 2024]

20. Gouin, J-P., et al. (2012), 'Stress, Negative Emotions, and Inflammation', in Decety, J. and Cacioppo, J. (eds), *The Oxford Handbook of Social Neuroscience*. Oxford: Oxford University Press, pp.815–829.

21. Canfield, J. (2005), *The Success Principles: How to Get from Where You Are to Where You Want to Be*. New York: HarperCollins

22. Connor-Savarda, B-N. (2023), 'The Science Behind Emotional Energy: Exploring the Vibrations of Our Emotional World', *Emotional Intelligence Magazine*: www.ei-magazine.com/post/the-science-behind-emotional-energy-exploring-the-vibrations-of-our-emotional-world [Accessed 26 September 2024]

23. Hawkins, D.R. (2014), *Power vs. Force: The Hidden Determinants of Human Behavior*. London: Hay House

24. *Ibid*

25. Hawkins, D.R. (2014), *Letting Go: The Pathway of Surrender*. London: Hay House

26. *Ibid*

27. Wineburg, S. (1987), 'The Self-Fulfillment of the Self-Fulfilling Prophecy: A Meta-Analysis', *Educational Researcher*, 16(9): 28–37.

Chapter 5: Your Environment

1. Schulz, J. (2017), 'Emotions are contagious: Learn what science and research has to say about it', Michigan State University Extension: https://www.canr.msu.edu/news/emotions_are_contagious_learn_what_science_and_research_has_to_say_about_it [Accessed 26 September 2024]

2. Harris, M.A. (2019), 'The Link Between Self-Esteem and Social Relationships: A Meta-Analysis of Longitudinal Studies', *Journal of Personality and Social Psychology*, 119(6):1459–1477.

3. Van Baaren, R., et al. (2009), 'Where is the love? The social aspects of mimicry', *Philos Trans R Soc Lond B Biol Sci*, 364(1528): 2381–9.

4. Spears, R. (2021), 'Social Influence and Group Identity', *Annual Review of Psychology*, 72: 367–390.

5. Peirce, P. (2009), *Frequency: The Power of Personal Vibration.* Portland, OR: Atria Books/Beyond Words

6. McMains, S. and Kastner, S. (2011), 'Interactions of top-down and bottom-up mechanisms in human visual cortex', *J Neurosci*, 31(2): 587–97.

7. Gosling, S.D., et al. (2002), 'The Psychology of Home Environments', *Perspectives on Psychological Science*, 10(3): 346–56.

8. Berridge, K.C. and Robinson, T.E. (2016), 'Liking, wanting, and the incentive-sensitization theory of addiction', *Am Psychol*, 71(8): 670–679.

9. Duhigg, C. (2012), *The Power of Habit: Why We Do What We Do in Life and Business.* New York: Random House Publishing Group

10. Adam, H. and Galinsky, A.D. (2012), 'Enclothed cognition', *Journal of Experimental Social Psychology*, 48(4): 918–925.

11. Gurney, D.J., et al. (2016), 'Dressing up posture: The interactive effects of posture and clothing on competency judgements', *British Journal of Psychology*, 108(2): 436–451.

12. Travers, C. (2021), 'Why theta waves are so healing + how to generate them more often', mbg health: www.mindbodygreen.com/articles/theta-waves [Accessed 26 September 2024]

13. Rivera Otero, J.M., et al. (2023), 'Emotions and Media: Emotional Regime and Emotional Factors of Selective Exposure', *Social Sciences*, 12(10): 554.

14. Haynes, T. (2018), 'Dopamine, Smartphones & You: A battle for your time', *Science in the News* (Harvard University): http://sitn.hms.harvard.edu/flash/2018/dopamine-smartphones-battle-time/ [Accessed 26 September 2024]

15. Hart, M. (2021), 'How parents can support kids' mental health during Covid-19', Unicef USA: https://www.unicefusa.org/stories/how-parents-can-support-kids-mental-health-during-covid-19 [Accessed 26 September 2024]

16. Moody, R. (2024), 'Screen time statistics: average screen time by country', comparitech: https://www.comparitech.com/tv-streaming/screen-time-statistics/ [Accessed 26 September 2024]

17. Nakshine V.S., et al. (2022), 'Increased Screen Time as a Cause of Declining Physical, Psychological Health, and Sleep Patterns: A Literary Review', *Cureus*, 14(10): e30051.

18. Brown, C. (2023), 'How Excessive Screen Time Negatively Impacts Our Health', Companion Link Software: www.companionlink.com/blog/2023/07/how-excessive-screen-time-negatively-impacts-our-health/ [Accessed 27 September 2024}

Chapter 6: Your Decisions

1. Hardy, D. (2011), *The Compound Effect*. Boston: Da Capo Press.

Chapter 7: Perfection Is a Scam

1. Wu, D., et al. (2017), 'Perfectionism mediated the relationship between brain structure variation and negative emotion in a nonclinical sample', *Cogn Affect Behav Neurosci*, 17: 211–223.

2. *Ibid*

Chapter 9: Making Setbacks Work for You

1. Canfield, J. (2005), *The Success Principles: How to Get from Where You Are to Where You Want to Be*. New York: HarperCollins.

Chapter 10: Your Future Self Maintenance Plan

1. Hyatt, M. (2022), '5 reasons why you should commit your goals to writing', Full Focus: https://fullfocus.co/5-reasons-why-you-should-commit-your-goals-to-writing/ [Accessed 26 September 2024]

2. Murphy, M. (2018), 'Neuroscience explains why you need to write down your goals if you actually want to achieve them', *Forbes*: www.forbes.com/sites/markmurphy/2018/04/15/neuroscience-explains-why-you-need-to-write-down-your-goals-if-you-actually-want-to-achieve-them/?sh=129e34707905 [Accessed 26 September 2024]

3. LePera, N. 'How to get the most out of future self journaling', The Holistic Psychologist: https://theholisticpsychologist.com/future-self-journaling/ [Accessed 26 September 2024]

4. University of Rochester Medical Center Health Encyclopedia, 'Journaling for Emotional Wellness': https://www.urmc.rochester.edu/encyclopedia/content.aspx?ContentID=4552&ContentTypeID=1 [Accessed 26 September 2024]

Acknowledgments

I'm filled with immense gratitude as I reflect on the journey of bringing this book to life. It's been a labor of love, and I owe so much to the beautiful people who have supported me along the way.

To Kate, thank you for believing in me all those years ago, even before I saw my own light. You have been more than just an agent; you've been my editor, my friend, my ally, and my biggest advocate. Your unwavering support, your willingness to go above and beyond, and your genuine belief in this book have meant more to me than words can express.

To my incredible Hay House team – Michelle, Amy, Helen, Debra, Grace, and everyone else who had a hand in this book – thank you for believing in me and for being my first publisher. Hay House is a standout company, and I feel so aligned with your values. I feel honored to be a Hay House author, and I'm deeply grateful for the opportunity to create this book with you.

To Jenna, thank you for helping my ideas to take shape and for eagerly diving into research with tight deadlines. Your support and editing skills have been invaluable.

To my soon-to-be husband, Ben, thank you for being my HM (Hydration Manager) during those long writing days; your humor and love have kept me going. Jokes aside, you truly are my rock, and I love you more than you know. I can't wait to marry you just a few months after this book is published.

To Mom and Dad, for your endless encouragement throughout my career. Mom, you truly set me on this path when you handed me *The Success Principles* by Jack Canfield all those years ago, and it's so special that our journeys have intertwined in this way. Dad, thank you for loving me unconditionally throughout every phase of my journey.

To my big sister, my favorite person in the world, thank you for being there every step of the way. You have been my biggest cheerleader from day one and I love you so much.

And lastly, to my readers and subscribers: thank you. You have been a vital part of my journey to becoming my Future Self. Thank you for allowing my words and voice to be a part of your life. I feel deeply blessed to have you here.

Love,
Mimi

About the Author

Mimi Bouchard is a trailblazing entrepreneur, innovator, and investor, and the founder of the Activations app, an eight-figure business that's redefined personal growth with a motivational alternative to traditional meditation. With Activations, Mimi offers a dynamic, science-backed method to help users transform their mindset and unlock their full potential.

Nearly a decade ago, Mimi radically transformed her life, moving from depression and financial struggle to abundance and fulfillment by embodying her 'Future Self.' As a leading motivational voice for women worldwide, Mimi's pragmatic approach and proven strategies inspire thousands to manifest their dreams with confidence and clarity. Her no-nonsense advice and emphasis on actionable results have made her a trusted mentor for those ready to make a profound change.

www.mimibouchard.com

www.activations.com

We hope you enjoyed this Hay House book. If you'd like to receive our online catalog featuring additional information on Hay House books and products, or if you'd like to find out more about the Hay Foundation, please contact:

Hay House LLC, P.O. Box 5100, Carlsbad, CA 92018-5100
(760) 431-7695 or (800) 654-5126
www.hayhouse.com® • www.hayfoundation.org

Published in Australia by:
Hay House Australia Publishing Pty Ltd
18/36 Ralph St., Alexandria NSW 2015
Phone: +61 (02) 9669 4299
www.hayhouse.com.au

Published in the United Kingdom by:
Hay House UK Ltd
1st Floor, Crawford Corner,
91–93 Baker Street, London W1U 6QQ
Phone: +44 (0)20 3927 7290
www.hayhouse.co.uk

Published in India by:
Hay House Publishers (India) Pvt Ltd
Muskaan Complex, Plot No. 3,
B-2, Vasant Kunj, New Delhi 110 070
Phone: +91 11 41761620
www.hayhouse.co.in

Let Your Soul Grow

Experience life-changing transformation—one video at a time—with guidance from the world's leading experts.

www.healyourlifeplus.com

activations

You can change your entire life in 3 months. Start now.

Download the Activations app today

Unlock 3 months free by going to www.activations.com/book or scanning the QR code below

$90 VALUE!

100% risk free, money-back guarantee

It's not meditation, it's activation.

CONNECT WITH
HAY HOUSE
ONLINE

🌐 hayhouse.co.uk   **f** @hayhouse

📷 @hayhouseuk   𝕏 @hayhouseuk

▶ @hayhouseuk   ♪ @hayhouseuk

'*The gateways to wisdom and knowledge are always open.*'

Louise Hay